W9-BRV-686

OLD TESTAMENT READING GUIDE

The Books of

ZEPHANIAH, NAHUM, HABAKKUK, LAMENTATIONS, OBADIAH

Introduction and Commentary

by

George T. Montague, S.M.
St. Mary's University
San Antonio, Texas

THE LITURGICAL PRESS ~ Collegeville, Minnesota

CONTENTS

English version of Zephaniah, Nahum, Habakkuk, Lamentations, Obadiah, copyrigh
© 1961 by Confraternity of Christian Doctrine, Washington, D.C. Used with permission. All rights reserved.

Nihil obstat: John Eidenschink, O.S.B., J.C.D., *Censor deputatus. Imprimatur*
✠ Peter W. Bartholome, D.D., Bishop of St. Cloud. August 15, 1967.

Typography and layout by the North Central Publishing Company, St. Paul, Minn
Printing and binding by Webb Publishing Company, St. Paul, Minn.

Copyright 1967 by The Order of St. Benedict, Inc., Collegeville, Minn. Printed in
U.S.A.

THE BOOK OF ZEPHANIAH

Introduction

The historical setting

The period which sets the stage for the first three prophets studied in this number of ORTG is the mid-seventh century B.C. — the decades that witnessed the greatest expansion and then the death-agony of Assyria, an empire that had stood mightily for nearly five centuries and at its apogee had wiped out the Northern Kingdom of Israel and then subjugated Judah to a long vassaldom. Hezekiah's attempt to wrest himself free from Ashur's grip failed, and his son Manasseh who succeeded him at an early age gave up all resistance and committed himself and the nation to the Assyrian overlord (2 K 21:1). From a human point of view there was little else to do: Assyria during this period extended its empire to the greatest dimensions; Esarhaddon (681-669), who succeeded his murdered father Sennacherib, proved to be an able and aggressive leader by triumphing even over Egypt, the one political hope to which a Judean king might look, as Hezekiah had done, for help against the colossus to the north.

The policy of Manasseh in internal affairs was a reversal of that of his father and a return to that of Ahaz, which had been condemned by Isaiah. The work of reform was entirely abandoned. Not only did the efforts at centralizing Yahweh-worship in Jerusalem fall apart through the king's restoring the local shrines, but all kinds of pagan cults and practices were permitted, even that of sacred prostitution which went unchecked in the Temple itself. The people not only aped foreign fashions, but were being mesmerized by the occult arts, divination and magic, then popular in Assyria (Zeph 1:8). Human sacrifice returned, Mannasseh himself setting the example (2 K 21: 3-7; 23:4-7). It was not that Yahwism was suppressed; it was simply being volatilized by an undiscerning integration with pagan worship which at its best would have left Yahweh at the head of a local pantheon (Zeph 1:9). The uniqueness and the demands of Yahweh's law were consequently ignored, resulting in new outbreaks of violence and injustice, coupled with a complacency that Yahweh would not and even could not do anything about it (Zeph 1:12; 3:1-7). The voice of prophecy, for the first time since the rise of the prophetic movement, was effectively silenced, apparently through the very simple policy of liquidating all dissenters (2 K 21:16).

The unscrupulousness of Manasseh's reign was matched only by its length — nearly half a century (687-642). His son Amon (642-640) continued his policies but was assassinated after a two years' reign by elements of the palace household, presumably of anti-Assyrian sentiment (2 K 21:19-24). But the time was not yet ripe for a complete break with the overlord, and the "people of the land," a term used at this time for influential landholders, put the assassin to death and placed on the throne the king's eight-year-old son Josiah. We know practically nothing of the early years of Josiah' reign; we may presume that the government was in the hands of advisers who may at best have hoped for independence but in practice followed a pro-Assyrian policy, attempting no serious reform of the abuses that had by now become well entrenched at every level of public and private life.

The Prophet Zephaniah

The title to the Book of Zephaniah tells us that the prophet exercised his ministry during the reign of Josiah. The tone of his oracles indicates that they were uttered during the early years of Josiah's regency, before the new king undertook his work of reform. (2 K 22:1-23:30; 2 Chr 34–35).

We know precious little about the life of Zephaniah. Great-great-grandson of Hezekiah, king of Judah (715–697 B.C.), he stood in the tradition of pure Yahwism and felt disgust over much that he witnessed at the royal court (Zeph 1:1). If he excoriates the court, it is at least a tribute to the improving situation that his voice was heard (even if not at once heeded) and that his oracles were somehow preserved. He was the first to break the long silence since Isaiah and Micah had spoken their last, more than two generations earlier under Zephaniah's illustrious ancestor.

The immediate situation which awakened Zephaniah to prophesy was, according to many scholars, raids by hordes of Scythians pouring out of Asia Minor and (according to Herodotus) ranging all the way to the Egyptian frontier (*History* I, 103–106). Zephaniah's oracles would thus be interpreting these invasions as harbingers of Yahweh's coming judgment upon the entire earth (Zeph 1:2-3). Jeremiah's early prophecies about the "enemy from the north" are also explained in the light of these raids (Jer 4; 6). Other scholars are less eager to accept the accuracy of Herodotus' description. And thus we are sure only of the fact that Zephaniah was using some invasion or attack to announce universal judgment.

Authenticity

With the exception of a few passages, the Book of Zephaniah is commonly regarded as the work of the prophet himself; its content does reflect the historical context of the regency of Josiah. Certain formulas of introduction (1:1, 8, 10, 12; 3:11, 16), explanatory glosses (1:4, 17; 3:5, 8, 10), and even variant readings (1:5; 2:2; 3:20), however, are best explained as the work of later editors. But historical criticism is much more circumspect today about relegating given passages to a later date merely because they reflect what is known to be characteristic of the later period. Thus, for example, the reference to the humble in 2:3, is not automatically to be termed postexilic simply because the movement of the "poor" reached its apogee then. Or again, the cosmic tableau traced by Zephaniah in 1:2-3 and 18, while certainly in keeping with apocalyptic thinking after the exile, is not in such complete discontinuity with preceding traditions as to demand a later date. By this time the flood story was well known, and both Amos and Micah painted their prophecies with cosmic colors (Amos 8:7-10; 9:1-7; Mi 4:11-13; 5:7, 8, 14).

Similarly, when the Philistine territory is promised to "the remnant of the house of Judah" (2:7), some critics hold that this can come only from exilic times; nevertheless, a promise made to Judah after an oracle against a foreign power is perfectly in context, and the remnant theme is as ancient as Amos (Amos 3:12; 5:15). Nor can any cogent reason be adduced to place the threats against Moab and Ammon (2:8-11) in the last days of Jerusalem.

It is not good historical method to adopt a system which ends in depriving of all originality a man recognized by his contemporaries as a prophet, and in this case the first voice of God to break a silence of 70 years.

However, certain passages fit the context poorly and seem to be imbued rather with the consolation theology of Second Isaiah. Such are the prediction of the conversion of the pagans in 2:11 and 3:9-10 and the two oracles which close the book (3:18-19 and 20). As for the two psalms of joy in 3:14-15 and 16-18a, these too seem to fit the exilic or postexilic times better, but there is less willingness among the critics to deny them to Zephaniah.

What is important to remember is that in the Catholic tradition of inspiration, the entire book is God's word, though anonymous scribes other than Zephaniah may have contributed to it. The essential concern of the reader is to grasp the message of the book as it stands.

The message and theology of Zephaniah

Like other prophets, Zephaniah announces the divine judgment upon the nations and upon Jerusalem herself. It is the "Day of the Lord." But more significantly than any other pre-exilic prophet, he describes the judgment in terms of cosmic catastrophe: all things will be swept from the face of the earth, man and beast, birds of the sky and fishes of the sea (1:2-3). His description makes twentieth-century man think of an atomic holocaust. How are we to understand the prophet's "cosmic judgment"? Is he predicting the end of the world? The liturgy has used his imagery to describe the "last judgment" in the Requiem Mass.

It is important first to realize that the classical Old Testament prophets had little concern for predicting events of the far-distant future. Theirs was the response of pure Yahwistic faith to the challenge of the moment. And while their prophecies were not always fulfilled in their own life-time, and often the fulfillment proved only to be partial, in their own mind there was no doubt that the present crisis was something God would soon resolve one way or another. Apocalypticism, with its imagery of cosmic battles in a distant future, arose only with the decline of prophecy.

As part of the judgment upon the present scene the prophets frequently introduced Yahweh as the Lord of creation who withdraws blessings or unleashes chaotic powers in the hope of winning conversion from his people. But when no response is forthcoming, the prophetic summons is given Israel to meet God, the creator (Amos 4:6-13; 8:9; 9:1-6). The implication is that divine judgment will involve a natural catastrophe, earthquake, flood, famine or pestilence. Sin, as the early chapters of Genesis seek to illustrate, merits and brings a return of primeval chaos.

Hosea casts the relation between nature and sin in poetic terms: when lawlessness and bloodshed run rampant, "The land mourns and everything that is in it languishes: the beasts of the field, the birds of the air, and even the fish of the sea perish" (Hos 4:3). On the contrary, on the day of reconciliation, the hungry child will ask for grain, wine, and oil; these in turn will ask the heavens for rain, and the heavens will ask the Lord — and he will respond (Hos 2:23). This is in part poetic, but it also is a condemnation of Israel's seeking the blessings of nature in the fertility rites of Canaanite worship rather than through Yahweh.

At other times, cosmic imagery is introduced merely to illustrate that the significance of some given political catastrophe is "world-shaking." Thus apparently the editor of Is 13 used the imagery of darkening stars, sun and moon, and the shaking of the heavens and the earth (Is 13:10-12) to fill out his prediction of the fall of Babylon; and Ezekiel does the same in his dirge over Pharaoh (Ez 32: 7-8).

Ancient prophetic thought understood better perhaps than we the solidarity of man with creation in his movement toward or away from God. When man turns from God, creation loses its meaning and turns upon man in hostility; through the pain and toil that creation causes him, it keeps reminding him of his more fundamental alienation from God and kindles a yearning for reunion with him. There is an inherent optimism in Judeo-Christian thought even in descriptions of the sinner's lot inasmuch as the natural effects of his sin are syndromes of his pathological state and signs beckoning him back to the Source of life. Thus the wrath of God upon the sinner is really identifiable historically with the natural results of man's sin and unwillingness to convert (cf. Is 9:17-18; Rom 1:24-32). When the Bible speaks of the disorder of creation, then, what it really means is that the objective order and beauty of creation sears the sinner with a judgment of disorder within himself; such a condition is like taking good food into an upset stomach — misery is certain.

What, then, are some practical points toward an understanding of Zephaniah? In 1:2-3, it is obviously an almost universal wickedness that merits the promised destruction of man and beast. Although Zephaniah seems to imply that all mankind will be destroyed, the context spells it out precisely as the wicked, as those who have fallen away from the Lord or do not seek him. In 1:14-18, the cosmic imagery almost totally dissolves into a description of the horrors of conquest by an invader. The prediction that God will make an end of all who live on earth must then be understood in this light. Everyone knows that an invader's sword makes no distinction between the good and the wicked. The prophet invites his people to convert and submit to the future as offered by Yahweh's law (3:5-8) before the invader's sword indiscriminately destroys all. If it comes to that, it will surely be the Lord's way, but it is not his preference.

The agent of this all-consuming judgment is the *fire of God's jealousy* (1:18; 2:8). Fire is a consistent element of theophany in the Old Testament, from the covenant vision granted to Abraham (Gn

15:17), through the appearances to Moses in the burning bush (Ex 3:2) and the pillar of fire by night (Ex 13:21-22), to the covenant theophany on Mount Sinai (Ex 19:18; 24:17). God is a consuming fire (Dt 4:24) and flames are the expression of his punishment (Gn 19:24; Lv 10:2) and jealousy: "a consuming fire, a jealous God" (Dt 4:24). The root meaning of the Hebrew word for *jealousy* is "to become red in the face." It is provoked by idolatry, which involves a breaking of the covenant union (Dt 32:16, 21) or by disobedience (Dt 4:24). Zephaniah's threat of God's consuming fire of jealousy follows a list of grievances Yahweh has against his people (1:18). God cannot abide infidelity.

But Zephaniah is best known for introducing the theology of the poor, the 'anawim. Like Isaiah, Zephaniah condemns the pride of nations (2:15) and teaches that salvation is possible only to a remnant. But Zephaniah is the first to identify this remnant with those who are imbued with poverty and lowliness of spirit (2:3; 3:12-13). Poverty here represents a genuine spiritual attitude of those "who take refuge in the name of the Lord." See the excellent study by A. Gelin, *The Poor of Yahweh* (Collegeville: The Liturgical Press).

Parallel to this, Zephaniah's theology of sin is more profound than mere moralizing. Behind the vices he condemns, he sees pride (1 16; 2:10,15; 3:11), the spirit of rebellion (3:2), lying (3:13), and especially a lack of trust, like that of a child who will not draw near his parent (1:12; 3:2). Zephaniah thus insists on sin as the aching rupture of personal relationship with God.

Over these basic strata of Zephaniah's prophecies lies a layer of universalism in the spirit of Second Isaiah, the author of chapters 40-55 in the Book of Isaiah (see *Old Testament Reading Guide* No. 20). There is a promise that the pagans will be converted (2:11), that they will worship Yahweh and serve him (3:9-10). To Israel is made the promise of complete restoration, the ingathering of exiles and renown and praise among the nations of the earth (3:18b-20).

If Hosea enjoys the honor of being the prophet of God's spousal love for his people, the Book of Zephaniah is not without a magnificent passage in which God is depicted as renewing Daughter Zion in his love and singing over her as at festvials (3:14-18). The future hope in Zephaniah is not the royal messianism of Isaiah; it is rather centered upon Yahweh's direct and perfect indwelling in the midst of a lowly and humble remnant. The joy this brings to Daughter Zion prepared the angel's "Rejoice" addressed to the Virgin of Nazareth, in whom the Son of the Most High came to dwell in the flesh a "mighty Savior" (3:14-17).

Outline of the Book of Zephaniah

THE BOOK OF ZEPHANIAH

Text and Commentary

I. THE DAY OF THE LORD FOR JUDAH
Zeph 1:2–2:3

1 The Word of the Lord which came to Sophonia,
   the son of Chusi, the son of Godolia, the son of
   Amaria, the son of Hezecia, in the days of Josia,
   the son of Amon, king of Juda.
2 I will completely sweep away all things
   from the face of the earth, says the Lord.
3 I will sweep away man and beast,
   I will sweep away the birds of the sky,
   and the fishes of the sea.
   I will overthrow the wicked;

No other prophetic genealogy matches this one in length.
The editor seems concerned to show that Zephaniah, despite
the Ethiopian name of his father, is of pure Judean race. The
content of the book indicates that the prophet exercised his
ministry largely during the regency of the young King Josiah
before the reform movement began.

2-3   The day of doom for Judah is introduced by a cosmic prelude of terrifying universality, recalling the deluge and the
oracles of Amos. As all creation shares in the justice of man,
so does it in the punishment of man's sin. A universal threat
to the cosmos can only announce God's impending judgment
upon man's sin, because sin merits a punishment more cata-
strophic than cosmic holocaust.

4   The object of this impending doom is primarily Judah,
virtually reduced, since Sennacherib's invasions, to its capital
city. There the idolatrous cults will be first swept away — to
the "last vestige," a phrase taken by some critics to refer to the
remnants of Baal worship not completely exterminated
5 by Josiah's reform of 621. Those devoted to Assyrian astral
worship (the "host of heaven") must perish too, as well as
those who adulterate their lip-service of Yahweh with a prac-

Gn 6:9ff
Amos 8:7ff; 9:1ff
Hos 2:20ff
Gn 3:17f
Hos 4:3

Jer 8:2; 19:13

I will destroy mankind
from the face of the earth, says the Lord.
⁴I will stretch out my hand against Juda,
and against all the inhabitants of Jerusalem;
I will destroy from this place the last vestige of Baal,
the very names of his priests,
⁵And those who adore the host of heaven on the roofs,
with those who adore the Lord
but swear by Melchom;
⁶And those who have fallen away from the Lord,
and those who do not seek the Lord.
⁷Silence in the presence of the Lord God!
for near is the day of the Lord,
Yes, the Lord has prepared a slaughter feast,
he has consecrated his guests.
⁸   On the day of the Lord's slaughter feast
I will punish the princes, and the king's sons,
and all that dress in foreign apparel.
⁹I will punish, on that day,
all who leap over the threshold,
Who fill the house of their master
with violence and deceit.
¹⁰   On that day, says the Lord,

6 tical reliance on Melchom, god of the Ammonites. Neither the apostate nor the indifferent will escape the judgment.

7 The "day of the Lord" picks up the prophetic theme introduced by Amos, but unlike the shepherd of Tekoa, Zephaniah's character as a cult-prophet, already suggested by his concern for pure Yahweh-worship, shows clearly in the framework of the liturgical feast by which he now depicts the day of the Lord. He cries for the silence befitting the presence of the Lord God in the temple. God has invited and prepared his guests for a great slaughter-feast. The guests are not identified; in Ez 39:17 they are the birds and wild beasts who will feast on the flesh and blood of the victims, an image developed in the Apocalypse. Others understand the guests to be the victims, as in the great religious

8 massacres of Elijah and Jehu, which purged Yahwism of the prophets and priests of Baal. In any case there is no doubt upon whom the judgment will descend: first of all upon the royal court where Assyrian influence has affected even the

9 manner of dress. "All who leap over the threshold" is an obscure phrase. It has been explained by some as alluding to the violation of justice by unlawful entry of homes. The more common explanation is that it refers to a pagan cultic

1 K 11:5,
33
2 K 23:13
Amos
5:18

Hb 2:20;
Zech 2:17;

Ap 8:1

Jer 46:10

Ap 16:6

2 K 9–10

A cry will be heard from the Fish Gate,
   a wail from the New Quarter,
   loud crashing from the hills.
11Wail, O inhabitants of the Mortar!
   for all the merchants will be destroyed,
   all who weigh out silver, done away with.
12At that time I will explore Jerusalem with lamps;
   I will punish the men who thicken on their lees,
Who say in their hearts,
   "Neither good nor evil can the Lord do."
13Their wealth shall be given to pillage
   and their houses to devastation;
They will build houses, but shall not dwell in them,
   plant vineyards, but not drink their wine.
14Near is the great day of the Lord,
   near and very swiftly coming;
Hark, the day of the Lord!
   bitter, then, the warrior's cry.

act reflected in part at least by 1 S 5:5. In ancient times the threshold was often thought to be the abode of spirits and demons. But the word *mitpan* may also stand for the platform of a throne, and thus the phrase would refer to the members of the court, who "mount the platform" to approach the king. In vv. 8-9 Zephaniah would be picturing the court during Josiah's regency. It is the ministers that are condemned rather than the king.

10 From the court the prophet's eye turns to Jerusalsm itself and describes the wailing that will come from the various quarters of the city. The predominance of the northern sections of the city (the Fish Gate was apparently in the north wall) indicates that the instrument of Yahweh's Day will be **11** an invasion. The location of the Mortar is not known with certainty, but it was the place of trade and industry, where the merchants, literally "the Canaanites" according to their popular title, "weighed out silver" (money was not yet in **12** common use). None can escape God's searching judgment; it will penetrate the recesses of the entire city and no retreat into darkness will be possible. Zephaniah's representation in art with a search-lamp takes its origin here. As will be the case with Jeremiah, the prophet's words fall heaviest on the vice of supine indifference. Wine that is not regularly stirred and poured from the vat becomes syrupy and sweet, and loses its proper taste; it "thickens on its lees" — an image of those who have committed everything to a here-

2 K 22:14

Hos 12:8;
Prv 31:24

Jer 48:11

> 15A day of wrath is that day
>   a day of anguish and distress,
>   A day of destruction and desolation,
>   a day of darkness and gloom,
>   A day of thick black clouds,
> 16   a day of trumpet blasts and battle alarm
>   Against fortified cities,
>   against battlements on high.
> 17I will hem men in
>   till they walk like the blind,
>   because they have sinned against the Lord;
>   And their blood shall be poured out like dust,
>   and their brains like dung.
> 18Neither their silver nor their gold
>   shall be able to save them
>   on the day of the Lord's wrath,
>   When in the fire of his jealousy
>   all the earth shall be consumed.

and-now enjoyment, implying that "God is dead," at least in his ability to act on the contemporary scene of human affairs. Some think that v. 13, which is derived from Amos 5:11, was inserted by an editor, since the Day of the Lord, in Zephaniah's mind, is coming too quickly for the figure to be in context here. But the image may also be understood in the sense that those who have already planted vineyards will not see their vintage nor drink their wine.

13 *Mi 6:15; Dt 28:30, 39*

14-18 With v. 14 begins a description of the Day of the Lord which has inspired the *Dies Irae*, attributed to Thomas of Celano and long used as the sequence at Requiem Masses. Zephaniah is heir to Amos 5:18-20 but has greatly expanded Amos' words. On that day, the cry of the warrior will not be one of victory but of anguish. It is a day black as night. The imagery of trumpet blasts and battle alarm, bloodshed and scattering of human brains suggests an enemy army putting the city to the sword. V. 18a has been interpreted as referring to the time when Psammetichus, king of Egypt, bought off the Scythians (Herodotus, *History I* 104). The destruction, as already announced in 1:3, is universal. The point of the whole passage is in v. 17: "because they have sinned against the Lord." God is a jealous God who cannot abide the turning of his people to other gods. He demands an exclusive adoration. The prophet's description of God's jealousy as fire echoes Dt. 4:24, "The Lord your God is a consuming fire, a jealous God," and prepares for Heb 12:29.

Is 2:6-22; 13:6-13; Ez 7:5-9 Jl 1:15; 2:1-2

Ex 20:5; 34:14; Dt 6:14

> For he shall make an end, yes, a sudden end,
>   of all who live on the earth.
> **2** Gather, gather yourselves together,
>   O nation without shame!
> 2 Before you are driven away,
>   like chaff that passes on;
>   Before there comes upon you
>   the blazing anger of the Lord:
>   Before there comes upon you
>   the day of the Lord's anger.
> 3 Seek the Lord, all you humble of the earth,
>   who have observed his law;
>   Seek justice, seek humility;
>   perhaps you may be sheltered
>   on the day of the Lord's anger.

God's intervention stems from his love which has made the people his own in covenant.

1-2   Not all is bleak in Zephaniah's message. The terrifying description of Day of the Lord introduces a call to conversion
3   directed to Judah, the "nation without shame." Like Amos, Zephaniah launches an appeal to "seek Yahweh," holding out not a guarantee nor even a promise but merely a "perhaps" regarding the possibility of escaping the impending doom. Neither Amos nor Zephaniah share the view that man's good acts can compel God to reward him by warding off temporal calamity. It is the "humble" whom the prophet addresses as he uses for the first time the word 'anawim to describe the lowly who seek spiritual poverty ('anawah). A seed is sown which will flower in a postexilic movement of the *poor*; themes proper to that movement will find expression in the psalms, in the New Testament (the Magnificat and the beatitudes), in the early Church, and in various bodies and congregations of the Christian era.

Amos 5:4-6, 14-15

Ps 25; 34; 37 Lk 1:46ff Mt 5:3; Acts 2:44

II. ORACLES AGAINST THE NATIONS
Zeph 2:4-15

The west: the Philistines—2:.4-7

The Philistine confederation originally consisted of five cities, four of which are named here. Gath is not mentioned, perhaps because it was already destroyed. The Philistine enmity dated back to the time of Samson and the first kings; it occasioned oracles by Amos (1:6-8), Isaiah (14:28-32) and

2 Chr 26:6

Jg 13–16

> 4For Gaza shall be forsaken,
>   and Ascalon shall be a waste,
>   Azotus they shall drive out at midday,
>   and Accaron shall be uprooted.
> 5Woe to you who dwell by the seacoast,
>   to the Cretan folk!
>   The word of the Lord is against you,
>   I will humble you, land of the Philistines,
>   and leave you to perish without an inhabitant!
> 6The coastland of the Cretans shall become
>   fields for shepherds, and folds for flocks.
> 7The coast shall belong
>   to the remnant of the house of Juda;
>   by the sea they shall pasture.

later by Jeremiah (47) and Ezekiel (25:15-17). Ashkelon
was captured and destroyed by Nebuchadnezzar in 604 B.C.
It was probably from here that a king named Adon wrote to
the Pharoah of Egypt appealing for aid against the Babylonian intruder. This letter, written in Aramaic, was found
in 1942 at Saqqare (Memphis). Ashdod was captured by
the Pharaoh Psammetichus I (666-610). Gaza remained
in Philistine hands until the end of the seventh century B.C.
But it had much to suffer, and was finally captured by Jer 25:20
Necho of Egypt within a generation after the prophecy of Jer 47:1, 5
Zephaniah. Ekron was the northernmost of the Philistine pen-
tapolis, near the beginning of the Valley of Sorek leading to
Jerusalem, but archeologists are not agreed as to its exact
site. At the time of Sennacherib's invasion, a coalition had
seized Padi, the pro-Assyrian king of Ekron, and handed him
over to Hezekiah. But after Sennacherib captured the city
and destroyed the conspirators, he forced Hezekiah to re-
lease Padi and restore him to power in Ekron. (See the map
in OTRG 5, 64-65).

The Philistines are called the "Cretan folk" because in Jer 47:4
Hebrew tradition they originally came from the isle of Crete; Amos 9:7
no archeological evidence, however, has been found that supports Philistine occupation of the island. Egyptian monu-
ments show Philistine warriors with headdress of upright
feathers.

7   Verse 7 is thought by many to reflect the situation of the
exile and hence to have been a later addition. However, the
basic idea of a remnant goes back to Amos and Isaiah, and

In the houses of Ascalon at evening
  they shall couch their flocks,
For the Lord their God shall visit them,
  and bring about their restoration.
8I have heard the revilings uttered by Moab,
  and the insults of the Ammonites,
When they reviled my people
  and made boasts against their territory.
9Therefore, as I live, says the Lord of hosts,
  the God of Israel,
Moab shall become like Sodom,
  the land of Ammon like Gomorra:
A field of nettles and a salt pit
  and a waste forever.
The remnant of my people shall plunder them,
  the survivors of my nation dispossess them.
10Such shall be the requital of their pride,
  because they reviled and boasted against
  the people of the Lord of hosts.
11The Lord shall inspire them with fear
  when he makes all the gods of earth to waste away;
Then, each from its own place,
  all the coastlands of the nations shall adore him.
12You too, O Chusites,
  shall be slain by the sword of the Lord.

it is not unusual to suppose that a threat to a foreign na- Amos 5:15
tion should evoke a promise, not indeed to the faithless men Is 4:3; 7:3
of Judah but to the humble remnant Zephaniah has already
described (2:3).

The east: Moab and Ammon—2:8-11

Since the time of the Exodus and the conquest, Moab and Nm 22—25;
Ammon, kingdoms lying to the east of the Jordan and the Jg 10—11
Dead Sea, had been rivals of the Israelites. Often condemned Amos 1:13ff
by the prophets, they must pay the price for their taunts Is 15—16
and insults against God's people. The height of their opposi-
tion appeared at the time of the capture of Jerusalem by the Jer 48
Babylonians. This fact has led some scholars to date the pas- Ez 25:1-11
sage from the time of that event. But if such be true, one
wonders why there is no mention of Edom, since Edom
aroused bitter hatred by joining the Babylonians in invading Ps 137:7-9
and ravaging Judah.

11   The final verse, however, reflects the universalism of Second Isaiah and is probably postexilic. Not only Moab and Is 41:5;
Ammon, but the coastlands or islands too will adore Yahweh 42:12;
on home ground. 51:5

> 13He will stretch out his hand against the north,
>   to destroy Assyria;
> He will make Ninive a waste,
>   dry as the desert.
> 14In her midst shall settle in droves
>   all the wild life of the hollows;
> The screech owl and the desert owl
>   shall roost in her columns;
> Their call shall resound from the window,
>   the raven's croak from the doorway.
> 15Is this the exultant city
>   that dwelt secure;
> That told herself,
>   "There is no other than I!"
> How has she become a waste,
>   a lair for wild beasts?
> Whoever passes by her
>   hisses, and shakes his fist!
>
> 3 Woe to the city, rebellious and polluted,
>   to the tyrannical city!
> 2She hears no voice,
>   accepts no correction;
> In the Lord she has not trusted,
>   to her God she has not drawn near.

The south: Egypt—2:12

A truncated form of what was probably a longer oracle is directed against Ethiopia (Kush). Ethiopia here seemingly stands for Egypt, ruled by Ethiopians during the 25th dynasty (712–663 B.C.). The prophet has in mind the attempts of Egypt at this time to extend her arm of conquest toward Palestine and Syria.

Is 18—20
Jer 46
Ez 29—32

The north: Assyria—2:13-15

Zephaniah saves for the climactic position the arch-enemy which for a century had oppressed Judah. The description of Niniveh's desolation is particularly graphic. The word translated "columns" is elsewhere used for hand-wrought jewelry and may refer to the famous bas-reliefs of the Assyrian palaces. Nineveh's deep humiliation merely corresponds to the height of her pride and self-sufficiency, summed up in the proud boast which Second Isaiah will later put on the lips of Babylon. "Hissing" was a characteristic expression of bewilderment at catastrophe. Shaking the fist was probably a gesture of the passerby to ward off similar misfortune from himself.

Is 47:8, 10
Jer 19:8

3Her princes in her midst
   are roaring lions;
Her judges are wolves of the night
   that have had no bones to gnaw by morning.
4Her prophets are insolent,
   treacherous men;
Her priests profane what is holy,
   and do violence to the Law.
5The Lord within her is just,
   who does no wrong;
Morning after morning he renders judgment
   unfailingly, at dawn.
6I have destroyed nations,
   their battlements are laid waste;
I have made their streets deserted,
   with no one passing through;
Their cities are devastated,

Nineveh, weak after the death of Ashurbanipal (c. 633 B.C.), fell to a coalition of the Babylonians and Medes in 612 B.C. A description of her fall is given in Nahum. There is no sufficient reason, however, to consider our passage an addition after the event.

III. AGAINST JERUSALEM
Zeph 3:1-8

The city and her leaders—3:1-5

1 Having traced the judgment of God upon the nations around Jerusalem, Zephaniah's prophetic finger descends directly
2 upon the city. It is not her sins but her lack of sincere repentance and amendment that unleashes the prophet's threats. Zephaniah's complaints against Jerusalem are
3 echoed by Jeremiah. The members of the king's court and administration, "the princes," are rapacious; the judges not only neglect justice but use their office to devour the poor
4 utterly. The official prophets, as Jeremiah will also testify, are a fraud, unfaithful to their vocation; they are really betraying the city. The priests, the custodians of cult and of law, are here accused of doing violence to the "torah." ("Torah," as here used, was not a body of literature, but priestly instruction, a later, more systematic development of the earlier function of giving oracles; it was a communication of the revealed will of Yahweh as a guide for action.) Zephaniah's association of the priests with the false prophets as deceivers of the people prepares for Jeremiah's similar denunciations.

Amos 1—2

Jer 2:30
7:28
Ez 22:27
Mi 3:11
Jer 23:32
Jer 2:8
18:18
Hos 4:4-6
Jer 5:30-31
6:13

> with no man dwelling in them.
> 7I said, "Surely now you will fear me,
>   you will accept correction";
> She should not fail to see
>   all I have visited upon her.
> Yet all the more eagerly have they done
>   all their corrupt deeds.
> 8Therefore, wait for me, says the Lord,
>   against the day when I arise as accuser;
> For it is my decision to gather together the nations,
>   to assemble the kingdoms,
> In order to pour out upon them my wrath,
>   all my blazing anger;
> For in the fire of my jealousy
>   shall all the earth be consumed.
> 9For then I will change and purify
>   the lips of the peoples,

5   Against this almost universal corruption stands the justice of
Yahweh. From Jer 21:12 we know that the time of day for
dispensing justice was the morning.

Yahweh renders judgment in the sunrise itself, an image
of his stable control over nature and a symbol of his unfail-   Ps 19:12
ing justice in dealing with men.

Judgment on the nations: a lesson—3:6-8

The lesson implicit in the sequence of oracles above, is now
drawn: the example of Yahweh's judgment on the pagan
nations was meant to lead Judah to repentance, but she did
8   not learn the lesson. We expect a threat to be pronounced
on Judah, but instead the perspective turns once again to
the universal judgment of the nations and the cosmic holocaust
in the "fire of my jealousy." It is the same image that con-   Zeph 1:18
cluded the section above on the universal judgment.

IV. PROMISES
Zeph 3:9-20

Conversion of the nations—3:9-10

The universalism of judgment melts into a universalism of
mercy, surprising for pre-exilic prophecy, and more in keep-
9   ing with the perspectives of Second Isaiah. Isaiah, at his call-   Is 6:5
ing, had bewailed the uncleanness of his own lips and that of
his people. The uncleanness of the nations lies not so much in

That they all may call upon the name of the Lord,
    to serve him with one accord;
10From beyond the rivers of Ethiopia
    and as far as the recesses of the North,
    they shall bring me offerings.
11   On that day
You need not be ashamed
    of all your deeds,
    your rebellious actions against me;
For then will I remove from your midst
    the proud braggarts,
And you shall no longer exalt yourself
    on my holy mountain.
12But I will leave as a remnant in your midst
    a people humble and lowly,
Who shall take refuge in the name of the Lord:
13   the remnant of Israel.
They shall do no wrong
    and speak no lies;
Nor shall there be found in their mouths
    a deceitful tongue;

10 their languages as in their calling upon other gods. But God will one day "turn over for the peoples a pure lip," a universal conversion to Yahwism, to serve him (in Hebrew, "with one shoulder"), suggesting common effort, as the LXX understood by translating "under one yoke." From the southern and the northern limits of the known world, an offertory procession comes to Yahweh. The conversion of the Ethiopians was foretold by Isaiah.

Is 18:7;
19:18-25;
45:14

The remnant of Israel, lowly and secure—3:11-13

11 For Israel herself, the ideal promised in 2:3 will be realized. God will one day remove from the city the "proud braggarts" and the holy mountain will no longer be a place for self-exaltation. For Zephaniah, the essence of sin is pride; in this judgment he shows himself a faithful disciple of Isaiah.

Is 2:11-17

12 The remnant, consequently, which will be of God's making, will be humble and lowly. For the first time the remnant is described in terms of the poor. While material poverty was never hailed as an ideal, in practice the "poor man" was the one whose covenant rights were most often violated; he had no refuge or defense but in Yahweh, and thus gradually he came to typify the just and the pious. This prepared for Zephaniah's identification of the remnant with the poor and lowly — titles certainly indicative of a spiritual attitude before

> They shall pasture and couch their flocks
>   with none to disturb them.
> 14Shout for joy, O daughter Sion!
>   sing joyfully, O Israel!
> Be glad and exult with all your heart,
>   O daughter Jerusalem!
> 15The Lord has removed the judgment against you,
>   he has turned away your enemies;
> The King of Israel, the Lord, is in your midst,
>   you have no further misfortune to fear.
> 16On that day, it shall be said to Jerusalem:
>   Fear not, O Sion, be not discouraged!
> 17The Lord, your God, is in your midst,
>   a mighty savior;
> He will rejoice over you with gladness,
>   and renew you in his love,
> He will sing joyfully because of you,
> 18   as one sings at festivals.
> I will remove disaster from among you,
>   so that none may recount your disgrace.

God and men. This verse represents the Old Testament's best description of spiritual poverty; it was surpassed only by the teaching and the example of Jesus.

Mt 5:3
Lk 9:58

13   These "poor" will attain genuine holiness. The idea parallels that of Jeremiah, who prophesies that in making the New Covenant God will achieve (finally) a genuine, interior holiness in his people. What was considered only a possibility in 2:3 is here promised as a certainty. The Apocalypse finds this imagery fulfilled in those gathered around the Lamb on the heavenly Mount Zion. The promise closes with the tender pastoral image of peace and everlasting security.

Jer
31:31-34

Ap 14:5
Mi 4:4

Two psalms of joy—3:14-18a

To the preceding promises the author, or more probably a redactor imbued with the theology of Second Isaiah, has attached two brief psalms, the first of which celebrates the enthronement of Yahweh in Zion. "Daughter Zion," "Israel," and "Daughter Jerusalem" all express the same reality. Originally used for a town near to and dependent upon a walled city, "daughter" came to stand for the community as such, here for all Israel concentrated in its capital. In Zech 9:9 the command to rejoice announces the Messiah; it is picked up by Luke in the annunciation to Mary. The presence of en-

Is 54:1

14

Ps 47; 48;
95—99

Jg 1:27

Lk 1:28

15

> 19Yes, at that time I will deal
>   with all who oppress you:
> I will save the lame,
>   and assemble the outcasts;
> I will give them praise and renown
>   in all the earth, when I bring about their restoration.

emies in Jerusalem was a judgment of the Lord; when the
Lord is once again within her, there will be no further misfortune to fear or (according to the LXX) to experience.

16   In the present text, there is a new start in v. 16. The expression, "On that day it shall be said to Jerusalem," may
be due to an editor, since the theme beginning with "Fear
not . . ." is closely connected with the preceding. It is more
likely, however, that two separate psalms, similar in content and form, were joined together. The basic message is the
same: Zion must no longer give way to fear or discourage-   Is 13:7
17   ment (in Hebrew, "let not your hands droop"). For the
Lord, as the hero who saves, as the Bridegroom who re-
joices on meeting his bride, will renew her in the fervor of
first love. (The LXX reading is to be preferred to the Hebrew,   Is 62:5
which has "He will be silent in his love"; perhaps this reflects the scruple of a scribe who knew God's love was not
always manifest in loud singing.) It is no longer necessary to
lead her into the desert to achieve this renewal; it will be   Hos 2:16,
18   done by the Lord in her *midst (beqirbek)*. To God is even   21
attributed joyous singing as on festivals. While theologically
the change must be said to take place in the bride, yet because it proceeds from Yahweh's renewing grace, the joy of   Lk 15:7
rediscovered love is attributed to him.

    The points of contact between Lk 1:26-38 and Zeph
3:14-18 are so numerous that many scholars think the evan-
gelist (or his underlying source) built the account of the Annunciation to Mary intentionally upon this hymn of messianic
joy: "Rejoice," "fear not," "The Lord in your midst (with
you, in your womb)" as "King" and "Savior." The term
beqirbek, which in Zeph 3:17 means "in your midst," can
also mean "in your womb," the sense in which Luke actual-   Gn 25:22
ized on the person of Mary the indwelling of the Lord promised in Zephaniah.

The great homecoming—3:18b-20

    The concluding section of the book, in a mixed and repetitive
style, reflects a historical situation later than that of the

20At that time I will bring you home,
    and at that time I will gather you;
For I will give you renown and praise,
    among all the peoples of the earth,
When I bring about your restoration
    before your very eyes, says the Lord.

prophet Zephaniah, since it assumes the fall of Jerusalem
and the exile. Three of the elements of exilic and postexilic
eschatology appear: destruction of enemies, ingathering of   Is 40:11
the diaspora, and return to the holy land.

The description closely parallels Mi 4:6-10 with the added
note of Israel's praise and renown among the nations as projected in Dt 26:19. All this will happen so openly as to silence
any doubt. The prophecy had a partial fulfillment in the return
of the exiles from Babylon. Christian tradition has understood
it, like the promise of 3:9-10, as fulfilled in the Church, the
"Israel of God," and finally to be consummated at the parousia   Gal 6:16
in the heavenly Jerusalem.   Ap 21; 22

THE BOOK OF NAHUM

Introduction

The historical setting

The shadow of Assyria's sword had lain across the land of Judah
ever since King Ahab of Israel had joined an anti-Assyrian coalition
and engaged Shalmaneser III in battle at Qarqar in 854 B.C. A few
years later Jehu of the Northern Kingdom became the first of a long
series of Israelites and Judaean kings to pay tribute to the expanding
colossus to the north. In 721 Assyria's Sargon II wiped out the Northern Kingdom completely and deported thousands of Israelites. The
Southern Kingdom fared little better, though Jerusalem was spared
by the sudden retreat of Sennacherib. The long reign of Mannaseh
(687–642) was one of groveling servility to the Assyrian overlord;
during it Esarhaddon entered Egypt and conquered Memphis in 671,
and his son Ashurbanipal marched southward up the Nile, captured
and destroyed Thebes in 663. But by the time young King Josiah
entered his regency (640), Assyria was on its way to decline and
Zephaniah could prophesy the downfall of Judah's century-old oppressor (Zeph 2:13-15).

The hope for this long-awaited day was fanned by subsequent
events, and what was only a short oracle in Zephaniah became a book
with Nahum. The judgment of God was about to descend upon Nineveh, the city on the banks of the Tigris which Sennacherib had made
the capital, and Ashurbanipal a center for artists and writers.

History reports the downfall of Nineveh in the following way. In
616 the emerging Babylonians took possession of the Middle Eu-
phrates valley, an area which the Assyrians had occupied for centuries. In 615 they attempted to take Ashur but were checked before
its walls. In the summer of 614, the Medes under Cyaxares took
Tarbisu, only three and one-half miles from Nineveh. They decided
against attacking the capital city itself (because of its heavy fortifications), turned instead on Ashur, and razed it after fierce combat. In
612, an alliance of Babylonians, Medes and Scythians marched on
Nineveh. It took weeks before the city capitulated. King Sinsharishkun
was killed, but some of the garrison managed to escape. At Harran
a new king, Ashuruballit, established himself and managed to hold

on to this shred of power until two years later (610) when the Scythians and Babylonians swept it away. Although Ashuruballit escaped to Carchemish, where the Egyptians came to his aid, both were crushed by the Babylonians in 605.

The occasion and date of Nahum's prophecy

Nahum's prophecy could not have been written before 663, the year of the fall of Thebes, which he describes in 3:8-10. The vividness of many of the details with which he paints the fall of Nineveh has induced some authors to say that he wrote after the city's fall in 612. However, the whole prophecy breathes a fresh and vigorous hope for the imminent collapse of the city.

Moreover, Nahum was a poet with a brilliant imagination, and the chariots whose veering and charging he describes, as well as the Assyrian life he reflects, were common knowledge among a people who had been under the heel of an overlord for a century. Finally, there is no hint whatever that the Babylonians might be more severe taskmasters than the Assyrians — as would be expected were the prophecy written after Babylon replaced Nineveh. And so, though some details may have been added later, such as 3:18-19 which seems to look backward to the event, the evidence points to composition shortly before the fall of Nineveh in 612.

Literary form; unity and authenticity

The prophecy of Nahum falls into the category of "Oracles against the Nations." These were never directed to the nations themselves but rather to the king and/or the people of Israel. Hence they were primarily salvation oracles. In the case of Nahum, the prophecies may have been composed as a kind of rogation liturgy in the temple to petition the speedy fall of Nineveh. The poetry of Nahum is among the finest in the Old Testament.

The section 1:2-10 presents special difficulties. It contains the remains of an acrostic poem somewhat upset by editing. In language and style it differs from that of the rest of the prophecy, and its theological and abstract approach contrasts with the vivid imagery of the rest. Moreover, in 1:4-5, Yahweh's wrath extends to Bashan, Carmel and Lebanon, whereas in the rest of the prophecy it rests only upon Nineveh. A widespread view, therefore, is that 1:2-10 is the work of a later hand; but it may just as well have been an earlier work incorporated by the author. At any rate, it is important in that it gives the religious perspective for the rest of the composition. The exact order of the last verses of ch. 1 and the first verses of ch. 2 is likewise disputed. Finally, the last two verses of the book (3:18-19) have been regarded as a later addition, since they reflect the fall of Nineveh as an accomplished fact.

Nahum—the man and his message

Beyond the meagre evidence of his work, we know precious little about Nahum. His name, well suited to his message for Judah, means "comfort, consolation"; it appears in the superscription of his book but nowhere else in the Old Testament. Not even the location of his native town of Elkosh is known with certainty, though the best candidate is a site in southwestern Judah. The tone of his prophecy leads many modern scholars to believe that he was a cult prophet associated with the temple in Jerusalem. He is certainly an enthusiastic patriot, possessed of a vivid imagination and sense of graphic detail. Although it is not necessary to place him in Assyria as an eyewitness of the events he describes, the reader at times will feel he is viewing a full-color documentary of the fall of Nineveh.

Nahum's theology is simple and unqualified. He belongs to the theological current which stressed Yahweh's unilateral and undying covenant with his people. God might be angry with his elect for a while, but he could never deliver them up forever, he could not allow the nation to be destroyed. Patriotism, for Nahum, was religion, and in his view of international affairs he must not have differed greatly from men like Hananiah or the 400 prophets who opposed Micaiah ben Imlah (Jer 28; 1 K 22). Nahum thus presents considerable contrast with his contemporary Jeremiah. The solitary priest-prophet of Anatoth does not even mention Assyria or Nineveh; he was unconsoled over the fall of the city and he grieved instead over the sins of Judah. If Nahum did not oppose Jeremiah, he was at least indifferent to his efforts, content to lead the people in a burst of vehement joy over the downfall of the enemy.

But the enemy was not just the enemy of Israel alone. Assyria had left blood in her wake all through the Fertile Crescent for a century, plundering everywhere to enrich her cities, and breaking her sworn word. These are crimes that cry out for the justice of God. While Nahum thinks of Yahweh's "justice" more in terms of his loyalty to his own people, there is nevertheless an underlying sense of universal justice which Nahum (or at least his final editor) assigns as the motive of God's punishing wrath.

No crime can go unpunished, and certainly not the atrocious, international crimes perpetrated by the Lion of Ishtar. God's wrath may be reluctant but it is inevitable (1:2-10). And, ironically, God' wrath appears in the case of Assyria as the natural issue of her atrocities. The punishment fits the crimes. In this sense there is a rebuke of militarism that prepares the statement of Jesus, "All who take the sword will perish by the sword" (Mt 26:52).

Nahum also introduces a cosmic dimension in his theophany of the Lord of judgment (Na 1:3-8). Some scholars think that he thus "historifies" certain elements from the ancient creation myths, that is, he identifies Nineveh with the cosmic adversaries who had been conquered at the beginning of creation. Drama to that effect, it is said, was re-enacted annually at the New Year festival. Although this view depends upon an interpretation of the temple liturgy which has not gained universal acceptance because of inadequate evidence, cosmic convulsions were an element of Biblical theophanies and were at times used to illustrate how "world-shaking" certain great historical events would prove to be (Is 13:10; Ez 32:7).

A commentary on chapters 2 and 3 of Nahum was discovered among the Dead Sea Scrolls. It applied the prophecy to recent and contemporary affairs known to the community at a time long after the historical event Nahum originally had envisioned.

Nineveh in archaeology (see sketch p. 37)

The site of the city which was the object of Nahum's prophecy has long been identified with two huge tells on the east bank of the Tigris river, opposite the present city of Mosul. A plan of the ruins was made as early as 1820 by C. J. Rich. When P. E. Botta was appointed French consul of Mosul in 1842, he began excavating the northernmost tell of Quyundjiq, without much success, particularly because he found a more interesting and fruitful site about ten miles further north at Khorsabad; the latter turned out to be Dur-Sharrukin, the capital built by Sargon II (721-705 B.C.). In 1845 the Englishman Layard excavated a tell farther south called Nimrud; it proved to be another ancient Assyrian city, Kalakh. In December 1853 H. Rassam came upon the first reliefs of Ashurbanipal at Quyundjiq, and before long the famous library of Ashurbanipal yielded thousands of clay tablets. Excavations continued at the site during the nineteenth century, and then after a long interval, a series of campaigns through the years 1922-1932 was carried on with careful attention to stratigraphy; the original level of the tell was finally reached at about 82 feet from the surface. Evidence pointed to an occupation of the site as early as 5000 B.C.

The other mound, Nebi Yunus (the Prophet Jonas), is guarded by a mosque, a burial ground and a village which forbids excavation. It is only about half as large as Quyundjiq, which is a mile long, nearly a half-mile wide, and stands about 90 feet high, rising sheer from the plain on all sides.

At the major tell, excavations revealed a complex of temples and palaces; among them the temple of Ashurbanipal, the palace of Sennacherib and the ancient temple of Ishtar. The worship of Ishtar at Nineveh goes back to Akkadian times (2500–2300 B.C.). Goddess of love and war, she was to be venerated by the Assyrians especially as a warrior, fitting symbol of their history. In the center of the mound stood the temple of Nabu, god of writing. Nahum will speak of the "scribes" of Nineveh (Na 3:15).

An outer wall about eight miles in circumference enclosed both tells and a segment of the Khoser torrent which brought the city an ample water supply. Beyond this wall, a double outer wall protected the city to the east. Along the west wall ran the river Tigris, which today has altered its course to form a kind of bow, touching the northwest and southwest corners of the city wall. On the waterworks, see commentary below.

Outline of the Book of Nahum

1:1	Superscriptions
1:2-10	*Part One*: THEOPHANY OF THE LORD OF JUDGMENT
1:11–2:3	*Part Two*: BLESSINGS AND WOES
1:12-13	To Judah
1:11, 14	To Assyria
2:1, 3	To Judah
2:2-14	*Part Three*: THE ATTACK ON NINEVEH
3:1-19	*Part Four*: HER CRIMES HAVE CAUSED HER DOWNFALL
3:1-4	Nineveh then and now — and why
3:5-7	Yahweh's sentence upon Nineveh
3:8-10	Nineveh is no better than Thebes
3:11-13	Now it is Nineveh's turn
3:14-17	Do what she may, doom is inevitable
3:18-19	Dirge over the city

THE BOOK OF NAHUM

Text and Commentary

1 Oracle about Ninive. The book of
the vision of Nahum of Elcos.
² A jealous and avenging God is the Lord,
an avenger is the Lord, and angry;
The Lord brings vengeance on his adversaries.
and lays up wrath for his enemies;
³ The Lord is slow to anger, yet great in power,
and the Lord never leaves the guilty unpunished.
In hurricane and tempest is his path,
and clouds are the dust at his feet;
⁴ He rebukes the sea and leaves it dry,
and all the rivers he dries up.

Unlike the superscriptions of major prophets, Nahum's carries no indication pertaining to the date. In this it is like Joel, Obadiah, Jonah and Habakkuk; it is the only prophecy to be entitled a "book" and to carry two superscriptions. The first, "Oracle about Nineveh," well expresses the single theme of the work. The classification "vision" places Nahum's prophecies alongside Isaiah's and Obadiah's, which are also so designated. If the name, "Nahum," meaning "Comforter," is symbolic of the prophecy, it indicates that the prophet's work was a salvation oracle addressed to the king or people of Judah rather than to Nineveh directly. The location of Elkosh has not been identified with certainty. A late tradition places it at Al-Qush, near Nineveh; Jerome placed it in Galilee; the best candidate so far, based on an ancient tradition which squares well with the historical setting of the book, is the region of Beit-Jibrin in southwestern Judah. If this location is correct, Nahum came from the same region as his predecessor Micah.

Is 1:1;
Ob 5:1

I. THEOPHANY OF THE LORD OF JUDGMENT
Na 1:2-10

The book opens with a theophany describing Yahweh's awful might and imminent judgment. The historical tragedy

Withered are Basan and Carmel,
and the bloom of Lebanon fades;
5The mountains quake before him,
and the hills dissolve;
The earth is laid waste before him,
the world and all who dwell in it.
6Before his wrath, who can stand firm,
and who can face his blazing anger?

to follow is rooted in the prophet's conception of Yahweh as master of human affairs, as judge who will let no crime go unavenged. Verses 2-10 contain the fragments of an acrostic poem, the order of which has been disturbed by later editing. The original structure of the poem has been recovered at least from its beginning with the Hebrew letter *'aleph* down to the letter *nun* in verse 9.

2   The poem begins with a *credo* in two traditional attributes of Yahweh. God's jealousy is based on the covenant commitment expressing his own loving election of his people and their sworn agreement in return to shun other gods and to abide by the stipulations of his covenant. Yahweh's jealousy is recalled by Nahum not for the purpose of exhorting the people to fidelity — the frequent function of the theme elsewhere — but rather to ground the certainty of God's coming intervention in their favor. This is how Nahum understands the Deuteronomic theme of God's presence among his people as assured by his jealousy. Similarly, God's vengeance (affirmed by the triple *noqem*), is the attribute by which he actively intervenes to punish the enemies of his own chosen ones or to defend the interests of his temple. Being the visible manifestation of God's saving justice, it is something the persecuted man prays for and something which forms part of oracles of consolation addressed to the people of Yahweh. St. Paul will insist that the Christian must not take vengeance into his own hands but leave it to God. The wrath of God, at times by other prophets directed against their own people, is thought of by Nahum as directed against Israel's enemies.

3   Verse 3a is a theological refinement which interrupts the acrostic; it was probably introduced by a later editor to soften the vigorous statement of the preceding verse. It is nonetheless significant in that it depicts God's avenging anger as the last resort to which his universal justice leads him. The

Jos 24:19
Ex 20:5
Dt 4:24

Dt 6:15

Ez 25:14
Is 63:4
Jer 51:11

Dt 32:35
Jer 11:20
Ps 94:1
Is 61:2
Rom 12:19
Jer 3:5, 12
Ps 103:9

His fury is poured out like fire,
and the rocks are rent asunder before him.
7The Lord is good,
a refuge on the day of distress;
He takes care of those who have recourse to him,
when the flood rages;
8He makes an end of his opponents,
and his enemies he pursues with darkness.

guilty may escape punishment from man, but never from God.
In 3b the acrostic is resumed, describing the cosmic convulsions frequently associated with the theophanies of wrath.
According to some authors, Nahum historifies the ancient
creation myth by which the forces of disorder were conquered
at the beginning of time, a myth re-enacted at Mesopo-
tamian New Year festivals. Nahum would be applying this
imagery to an historical enemy, Nineveh. At any rate, the
primitive conception of Yahweh and of El Shaddai as a Ex 19:16-19
storm God re-emerges here in terms reminiscent of Sinai, of Jb 38:1;
Yahweh's answer to Job, and of other Biblical theophanies. 40:6
The clouds are the dust stirred up by Yahweh's feet as he Zech 9:14
4-5 strides to judgment. He is the God of the Exodus who dried
up the sea and the Jordan — a motif which Second Isaiah
will use in his description of the return from the Babylonian Is 50:2;
exile, joining with it the poetic imagery of conquest over the 51:10
primeval chaos. Bashan, east of the Jordan, is today largely
deforested; in Biblical times it was famous for its trees and Amos 1:2;
flocks. Along with Carmel and Lebanon, it would be the 4:1;
least likely to suffer the effects of drought. But it too withers, Mi 7:14
and the very pillars of the earth collapse, and all animate Jb 9:5f
6-7 creation with them. Obviously, no creature can oppose God's
power or the judgment of his wrath.

Fire is a favorite biblical figure for God's fury. In joining Mal 3:2;
the figure of fire to that of the splitting of rocks, Nahum is Jer 10:10
heir to Jeremiah who thus describes the effectiveness of the Jer 7:20
prophetic word: "Is not my word like fire, says the Lord, like
a hammer shattering rocks?" But it is not against his own Jer 23:29
people that Nahum evokes this world-shaking vision of hor-
ror. God's *hesed* or loving-kindness is pledged to his own; for Dt 5:9f
those who turn to him he is a refuge from the storm. The
Hebrew reads literally, "He knows those who have recourse to Jer 16:19
him," but the knowledge spoken of is one of active and loving
concern, as in Amos 3:2. God receives them not as strangers
but as his beloved children.

> 9What are you imputing to the Lord?
> It is he who will make an end!
> The enemy shall not rise a second time;
> 10As when a tangle of thornbushes is set aflame,
> like dry stubble, they shall be utterly consumed.
> 12For, says the Lord,
> be they ever so many and so vigorous,
> still they shall be mown down and disappear.
> Though I have humbled you,
> I will humble you no more.
> 13Now will I break his yoke from off you,
> and burst asunder your bonds.

8   Some versions take "with a flood" as modifying what follows, but our version renders an acceptable sense in keeping with the context. In Gn 1:2 darkness forms part of the primeval chaos; nevertheless it too depends upon God and can, poetically speaking, praise God. Here it is an instrument of Yahweh's vengeance and is easily equated with death.

Ps 104:20
Dn 3:72
1 S 2:9

9-10   The original acrostic would demand putting the third phrase of verse 9 first, but it is better to follow the order of the Hebrew text. In any case, the question is addressed to the foes of Yahweh. It can mean, "What are you thinking of Yahweh?" or "What are you plotting against Yahweh?" Verse 9 reads literally, "affliction will not arise twice." The thought seems to be that no second stroke of punishment on Nineveh will be necessary, since the destruction will be utter.

Hos 7:15
Dn 11:24

II. BLESSINGS AND WOES
Na 1:11—2:3

To Judah

12-13   Now follows a series of oracles alternately addressed to Judah and to Assyria. Judah's plight has been an affliction from Yahweh, but the end of it is promised. Breaking or loosing a yoke meant cutting or untying the thongs holding the two sides of the yoke together — a fequent Biblical image for liberation.

Jer 30:8
Ps 2:3

To Assyria

11   Replaced here in better context, this line is addressed to Assyria. No doubt "the scoundrel planner" is Sennacherib, who came from Nineveh to attack Jerusalem; in Nahum's view the Assyrian invader was warring against Yahweh himself.

> 11From you he came
>   who devised evil against the Lord,
>   the scoundrel planner;
> 14The Lord has commanded regarding you:
>   no descendant shall come to bear your name;
> From your temple I will abolish
>   the carved and the molten image;
>   I will make your grave a mockery.
>
> 2 See, upon the mountains there advances
>   the bearer of good news, announcing peace!
> Celebrate your feasts, O Juda,
>   fulfill your vows!

Micah, on the contrary, regarded Sennacherib as an instrument in Yahweh's hands punishing Judah and Samaria for their sins.

14   The masculine pointing of the 2nd person pronouns interprets this as addressed to the Assyrian king, Sin-shar-ish-kun, thus assuring him of no descendants, or to the people of Assyria personified, foretelling the end of the nation. Indeed it seems that the successor of Sin-shar-ishkun was not his son, but one of the higher officials. Other scholars point the words as feminine and understand them of the city of Nineveh. The patriot Nahum certainly expects more than the downfall of a dynasty. The Assyrians (and the Babylonians after them) were accustomed to destroying or carrying off the images and desecrating the temples of the peoples they conquered, thus demonstrating the powerlessness of the gods so insulted. Nahum now sees the same fate befalling Assyria, and it is Yahweh himself who executes it.

To Judah

1   The relaying of good news is pictured according to the ancient system of "telegraphy": a herald runs to a hilltop and shouts to another herald across the valley. The message "Peace" announces, in addition to the cessation of hostility, the return of prosperity and freedom. The image will be picked up by Second Isaiah. The messenger adds that Judah may now celebrate her feasts in pomp and joy, indeed she must do so in thanksgiving to Yahweh. The many vows made to Yahweh to obtain the enemy's downfall must now be fulfilled. The liturgical motif here supports the theory that Nahum was a temple prophet. The oppressor will now experience the fate he has so often meted out to others.

Is 13:2

Is 40:9;
52:7

> For nevermore shall you be invaded
>   by the scoundrel; he is completely destroyed.
> 3 The Lord will restore the vine of Jacob,
>   the pride of Israel,
> Though ravagers have ravaged them
>   and ruined the tendrils.
> 2 The hammer comes up against you;
>   guard the rampart,
> Keep watch on the road, gird your loins,
>   marshal all your strength!
> 4 The shields of his warriors are crimsoned,
>   the soldiers colored in scarlet;
> Fiery steel are the chariots
>   on the day of his mustering.
> The horses are frenzied;
> 5   the chariots dash madly through the streets
> And wheel in the squares,

3   The image of the vine for the people of God was a favorite
of the prophets. In a country whose economy depended largely on the vine and the olive tree, the image of a vineyard
ravaged by beasts or by storm offered a tragic but vivid image
of enemy oppression. There is a difference of but one conso-
nant between "vine" and "pride" in Hebrew. "The pride of
Israel" may simply be an equivalent of Judah, represented by
Jacob, but the hope for the restoration of the Northern Kingdom was also vivid in postexilic times and may well be expressed here.

Hos 10:1
Is 5:2-7,
Jer 2:21
Jer 48:32,
Ps 80:9, 14
Is 43:1

Is 11:12ff,
Zech 10:6ff

III. THE ATTACK ON NINEVEH
Na 2:2-14

2   Nahum's vivid, rapid-fire imagery sounds like a modern
journalist broadcasting an event as he witnesses it. The enemy
is poised like a raised sledge hammer ready to fall upon the
city. The prophet ironically taunts the city with his cries to
prepare, especially by bracing interiorly for the inevitable attack.

4   Whether there is special significance to the crimson color
of the shields is uncertain. Some have suggested that it describes blood dripping from the shields; others, that it refers
to leather facings of the shields dyed or anointed with red
oil; others, the reflection of the sun on the bright copper surface. Scarlet appears to have been the characteristic color
of the Babylonians and Medes (Xenophon, *Cyropedia*, VI,
4, 1), whereas blue or purple was that of the Assyrians.

Is 21:5

Ez 23:14
23:6
27:23

> looking like firebrands,
> flashing like lightning bolts.
> 6His picked troops are called,
> ranks break at their charge;
> To the wall they rush,
> the mantelet is set up.
> 7The river gates are opened,
> the palace shudders,
> 8Its mistress is led forth captive,
> and her handmaids, under guard,
> Moaning like doves,
> beating their breasts.
> 9Ninive is like a pool
> whose waters escape;
> "Stop! Stop!"
> but none turns back.
> 10"Plunder the silver, plunder the gold!"

5 The chariots are armored; those of the Medes may well resemble the chariots of the Assyrian king and his nobles, which we know from sculptures were covered with polished metal and in the sunlight would gleam with a brightness resembling fire. The words for "streets" and "squares" may also apply to fields outside the city walls, as would fit the sequence of the description better. The chariots impress the viewer with their speed and brilliance.

Jb 5:10;
Prv 24:27

6 The moment for storming the walls has arrived; the picked troops make the final onslaught. The exact nature of the mantelet is unknown; the Hebrew word which occurs only here in the Bible, means literally "coverer," suggesting a movable shelter protecting the besiegers. But it may also refer to the siege-machine and battering ram, of which examples are known from Assyrian reliefs.

7 Nineveh may not have had the colossal proportions given it by the book of Jonah, but it was a gigantic city by ancient standards, covering an area of 1800 acres; the outer walls were nearly eight miles in circumference. It lay on the east bank of the Tigris. The Khoser, a torrent coming down from the mountains to the northeast, cut directly through the center of the city and emptied into the Tigris. A series of dykes and dams controlled the waters of both these streams, and water was available in abundance for the complex system of moats and walls. In addition to the major wall that surrounded the city and its moat, there were to the east two outer walls, each about fifty-five feet in height, between which lay a

>   There is no end to the treasure,
>   to their wealth in precious things of every kind!
>   11Emptiness, desolation, waste;
>   melting hearts and trembling knees,
>   Writhing in every frame,
>   every face blanched!

moat about fifty-five yards wide. Exactly where in this complex the "river gates" to which Nahum refers were located is not known. The opening of these gates signified the fall of the city. See sketch, p. 37.

8   The meaning of the Hebrew word *huṣṣab* is uncertain. Translated "mistress," it may refer to the queen with the maidens of her court or, more probably to the goddess Ishtar, who would certainly have held more interest for Nahum, as apparently she did also for the Assyrian kings.

In this case the "handmaids" would refer to the temple prostitutes who devoted themselves to the worship of Ishtar and were called *Kadishtu* ("consecrated ones") or *Ishtari-tum* ("dedicated to Ishtar"). The cooing of doves is a Biblical figure for mourning. The beating of the breast was already in ancient times a gesture of grief, as appears also from the New Testament.

Is 38:14;
59:11;
Ez 7:16
Lk 18:13;
23:48

9   To the Assyrian generals who led the defense, the deteriorating situation must have seemed just as Nahum describes it: like a pool rapidly losing water. The loss of control of Nineveh's waterworks as dikes and dams crumbled before the enemy's bombardment was but the outward symbol of the rapid defection of the rank-and-file defenders, who were fleeing panic-stricken, deaf to the cries of their leaders.

Jer 46:5;
43:39

10   Nahum now invites the victors to plunder Nineveh's fabulous wealth, to which numerous Assyrian inscriptions testify. Booty from her many campaigns and the heavy tribute she imposed on the vanquished served to create an empire of incalculable wealth.

11-13   In the final strophe, Nahum shows how Assyria's cruel inhumanities upon all neighboring nations now come home upon her in revenge. "Emptiness, desolation, waste" have an assonance in Hebrew which cannot be rendered in English: *buqah umᵉbuqah umᵉbullaqah.*

The Babylonian Chronicle (line 45) reads: "The spoils of the city, more than could be numbered, they took for themselves and they (rendered) the city to a mound and

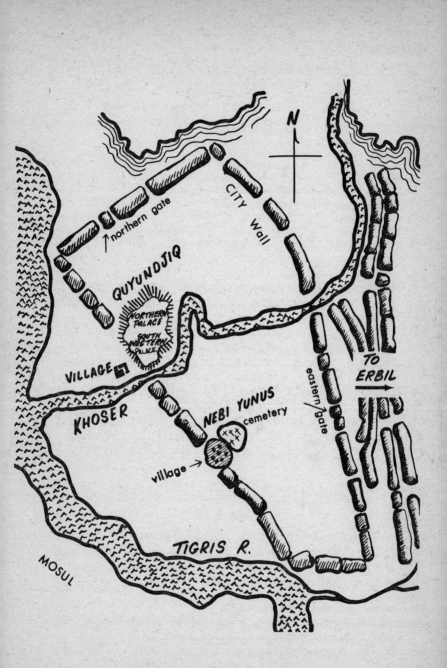

The Site of Ancient Nineveh

> 12Where is the lions' cave,
>   the young lions' den,
> Where the lion went in and out,
>   and the cub, with no one to disturb them?
> 13The lion snatched enough for his cubs,
>   and strangled for his lionesses;
> He filled his dens with prey,
>   and his caves with plunder.
> 14I come against you,
>   says the Lord of hosts;
> I will consume in smoke your chariots,
>   and the sword shall devour your young lions;

a ruin." "Writhing in every frame" is literally, "anguish in all loins." The loins are the seat of strength, and now the citadel of strength is gripped by weakness and pain similar to a woman's birth-pangs. The figure of the lion for Assyria is fitting not only in the general sense in which enemies of Israel were often represented, but because the lion was a favorite decorative symbol in Assyria.

Jb 40:16

Is 21:3

Jer 4:7
Zeph 3:3

14   The theological significance of Nineveh's downfall is again touched upon. Though the instrument of the city's destructoin may be the Medes instead of the Israelites, it is nonetheless Yahweh who is bringing it about. The oracular form used here will appear often in Jeremiah and Ezekiel to announce a punishment from Yahweh. "The cry of your (lit.) *messengers* will be heard no more," i.e., agents of the king sent to exact tribute or to enforce submission will no longer be heard, a reminiscence perhaps of the Rabshakeh incident in Hezekiah's time.

Jer 21:13
Ez 5:8

2 K 18:17,
19; 19:9,
23

IV. HER CRIMES HAVE CAUSED HER DOWNFALL
Na 3:1-19

From here to the end, the graphic description of the city's collapse continues, but with increased emphasis on the reason for it: Assyria's crimes. Six strophes, all addressed to Nineveh, sing out Nahum's exultation at the city's downfall.

Nineveh then and now—and why—3:1-4

The first strophe describes Nineveh as she was known in the ancient world, contrasts that condition with her plight at her destruction, and ends by assigning the reason for the tragedy.

Your preying on the land I will bring to an end,
   the cry of your lionesses shall be heard no more.
3 Woe to the bloody city, all lies,
   full of plunder, whose looting never stops!
2 The crack of the whip, the rumbling sounds of wheels;
   horses a-gallop, chariots bounding,
3 Cavalry charging,
The flame of the sword, the flash of the spear,
   the many slain, the heaping corpses,
   the endless bodies to stumble upon!
4 For the many debaucheries of the harlot,
   fair and charming, a mistress of witchcraft,

Mass atrocities were commonplace in ancient warfare, and Assyrian inscriptions show that her practices were surpassed by none. "A pyramid of heads in front of his city I erected. Their young men and women I burned in a bonfire" (Shalmaneser Monolith I, 16ff). "And they (the officers) put to the sword the inhabitants, young and old, of the towns of Sais, Pindidi, Tanis and of all the other towns which had associated with them to plot; they did not spare anybody among them. They hung their corpses from stakes, flayed their skins and covered (with them) the walls of the towns" (Ashurbanipal, ANET 295).

Esarhaddon describes a victory demonstration at Nineveh in these words: "I hung the heads of Sanduarri and Abdimil- 2 K 10:6-8 kutte around the neck of their nobles . . . to demonstrate to the population the power of Ashur, my lord, and paraded (thus) through the wide, main street of Nineveh with singers (playing on) . . . harps" (ANET 291).

Nahum evokes this history with one adjective: "bloody." Like so many powers striding to world domination, Assyria had made promises to weaker nations only to break them when expediency demanded. Finally, Assyria's plundering of cities and kingdoms is historically accurate. One example among many is the three statues of Pharaohs, unearthed in 1954, which must have been brought from Egypt by Esarhaddon. After describing his decapitation of Abdimilkutte, Esarhaddon boasts: "I carried off as booty: his wife, his children, the personnel of his palace, gold, silver, (other) valuables, precious stones, garments made of multicolored trimmings and linen, elephant-hides, ivory, ebony and boxwood, whatever precious objects there were in his palace, (and) in great quantities. I led to Assyria his teeming subjects, which

Who enslaved nations with her harlotries,
and peoples by her witchcraft:
5I am come against you,
and I will strip your skirt from you;
I will show your nakedness to the nations,
to the kingdoms your shame!
6I will cast filth upon you,
disgrace you and put you to shame;
7Till everyone who sees you runs from you, saying,
"Ninive is destroyed; who can pity her?
Where can one find any to console her?"
8Are you better than No-Amon
that was set among the streams,

could not be counted, (and) large and small cattle and don-
keys in great quantities" (ANET 291).

Nahum stigmatizes Assyria's character in three swift
strokes: "Blood, lies, and plunder!"

2-3   Picking up again his on-the-scene technique, Nahum im-
agines what the city's last day will be like—and his stac-
cato style suggests the bustle and uproar of battle. How
much of this actually occurred when Nineveh fell we do
not know, but the Medes and the Babylonians were not
known for clemency. The Stele of Nabuna'id compares the
ruin of Assyria to the effects of a cyclone.

4   The reason assigned for this bloody vengeance is the "debaucheries of the harlot," that is, her policy of seducing the
nations unto her own selfish ends. "Witchcraft" probably re-   2 K 9:22
fers to various charms and spells through which harlots
sought to entice men. The image of the harlot is used else-   Hos 2:5
where in the Old Testament for Israel herself or for Jerusa-   Ez 16:15
lem.

Yahweh's sentence upon Nineveh—3:5-7

The image of the harlot continues, but now it is Yahweh
himself who speaks and acts. The exposure to shame here described was the punishment in Israel for fornication and adul-   Jer 13:23,
tery. Yahweh is depicted as doing what bystanders would   26f
do to such women, namely, pelt them with filth. So frightful   Ez 16:36f
will be the sight of the razed city that passers-by will flee;   Hos 2:3, 9
no one left among the living will regret the fall of Nineveh.

Nineveh is no better than Thebes—3:8-10

8   Among the titles to Nineveh's historical pride was the conquest of her great rival Thebes (No-Amon, a form of Nut-

> Surrounded by waters,
>> with the flood for her rampart
>> and water her wall?
> 9Ethiopia was her strength, and Egypt,
>> and others without end;
> Phut and the Libyans were her auxiliaries.
> 10Yet even she went captive into exile,
>> even her little ones were dashed to pieces
>> at the corner of every street;
> For her nobles they cast lots,
>> and all her great men were put into chains.
> 11You, too, shall drink of this till you faint away;
>> you, too, shall seek a refuge from the foe.

Amen) in 663 by Ashurbanipal. The same fate is now turned on the Assyrian capital. The similarities are more than one. Like Nineveh, Thebes was situated on a great river; Thebes enjoyed the inundation of the Nile and most probably had a system of moats — since the Egyptians had used these as means of defense since the 19th century B.C. Like Nineveh, Thebes was an immense city whose fame extended all over the ancient world. In it stood the magnificent temple of Karnak, built to honor the patron god of the city, Amon.

9 At the time of its conquest by the Assyrians, Thebes was ruled by the twenty-fifth dynasty, which was Ethiopian. In addition to the resources from Nubia, the defenders had as allies Put (location uncertain) and the Libyans, her neighbors to the west.

10   Nahum's recollections are generalizations from a later generation. But they fit the context of Ashurbanipal's own description of his capture of Thebes: "Upon a trust(-inspiring) oracle of Ashur and Ishtar I, myself, conquered this town completely. From Thebes I carried away booty, heavy and beyond counting: silver, gold, precious stones, his entire personal possessions, linen garments with multicolored trimmings, fine horses, (certain) inhabitants, male and female. I pulled two high obelisks . . . the weight of which was 2,500 talents, standing at the door of the temple, out of their bases and took (them) to Assyria" (ANET 295). The bashing of babies and the ripping of pregnant women were common atrocities in ancient warfare, and one such instance is recorded of the Israelite Menahem. The nobles, according to Nahum's recollection, were carried off and lots were cast among the Assyrian princes for their possession.

2 K 8:12
Is 13:16, 18;
2 K 15:16
Amos 1:13

12All your fortresses are but fig trees,
    bearing early figs
That fall, when shaken,
    into the hungry mouth.
13See, the troops are women in your midst;
    to your foes the gates of your land are open wide,
fire has consumed their bars.
14Draw water for the siege,
    strengthen your fortresses;
Go down into the mud and tread the clay,
    take hold of the brick mold!

Now it is Nineveh's turn—3:11-13

11 Nineveh will drink of Yahweh's wrath till she is drunk and
12 helpless. Her fortresses, whether the outposts or the ram-
parts of the city, resemble the season's first figs, which are
13 eagerly plucked and fall without effort. The defending sol-
diers, in Nahum's view, are unable to act like men, so dis-
spirited will they be. As a matter of historical fact, Nineveh's defenses were formidable enough to dissuade the
army of Cyaxares from attacking it in 614. And in the actual
battle of 612 the defenders held out long and bitterly—a
fact which shows the prophecy was not written up after
the event. A layer of destruction debris, the main element
of which is charcoal, is the normal indication to archeologists of a destruction, since cities were usually razed. Use of
fire is indicated here in the burning of the bars.

Hab 2:16
Jer
25:15-27

Is 19:16
Jer 49:22

Do what she may, doom is inevitable—3:14-17

14 Essential to withstanding a siege was an adequate water supply. Excavations of fortified sites like Megiddo, Gezer and
Massada in Palestine have revealed enormous cisterns.
Sennacherib, in the Bavian inscription, tells how he directed
the water from eighteen wadies into the city by means of
an aqueduct. Nahum perhaps envisions the last-minute
strengthening of this system, just as Ahaz had done in face
of the Syro-Ephraimite threat. A supply of bricks would be
needed to keep the walls in repair, particularly from the effects of the enemy's battering rams. Excavations have shown
that the walls of Nineveh were fifty feet in width and wid-
ened to over 100 feet near the gates. Diodorus estimates the
height of the walls at 100 feet, an observation which gives
credibility to Sennacherib's boast that he made the walls
15 "mountain high" (Bavian inscription). At the very site of

Is 7:3

> [15]There the fire shall consume you,
>   the sword shall cut you down.
> Multiply like the grasshoppers,
>   multiply like the locusts!
> [16]Make your couriers more numerous than the stars,
> [17]   your garrisons as many as grasshoppers,
>   And your scribes as locust swarms
>   gathered on the rubble fences on a cold day!
> Yet when the sun warms them,
>   the grasshoppers will spread their wings and fly,
>   and vanish, no one knows where.

their wearisome labors, fire and sword will fall upon them. Excavations at Quyundjiq, one of the two major tells of Nineveh, have shown widespread destruction by fire. From the fortifications Nahum's view turns to the inhabitants and the defenders themselves; no matter how numerous they may be, and even if they swarm like a plague of locusts, the result will be totally futile. The "couriers" are merchants who go about trading, an important source of Nineveh's wealth. The "scribes" were probably government officials; their importance had been established in Assyrian life by Ashurbanipal, who employed them in copying ancient tablets and in amassing his great library. Excavations at Quyundjiq have revealed a temple to Nabu, god of writing in the very center of the tell. It is possible that in the latter days familiar to Nahum, the image of Nineveh was less that of a stalwart soldier than that of merchant and scribe.

"Grasshoppers" and "locusts" are practically interchangeable in the Bible, but the reference to the gregarious and flying phase indicates Nahum is thinking of the swarming of locusts. Certain kinds of locusts were considered a delicacy by the Assyrians (an Assyrian relief shows an attendant carrying locusts on a skewer). But their occasional swarming could be a devastating plague. Experiments, published by F. S. Bodenheimer in 1930, show that at 40° fahrenheit locusts are reduced to a state of torpor; they return to normal behavior when the temperature reaches about 70° and reach maximum excitation around 110°. Similarly Nineveh's population is huddled on her walls, but they will vanish as suddenly as a swarm of locusts that take wings at the rising of the sun. The spectator will see the Assyrians dispersed and deported to unknown destinations. The desert locust is now known to migrate as far as 1,200 miles from its native habitat.

Ex 10:12
Jl 2:4-9

18Alas! how your shepherds slumber, O king of Assyria,
    your nobles have gone to rest;
Your people are scattered upon the mountains,
    with none to gather them.
19There is no healing for your hurt,
    your wound is mortal.
All who hear this news of you
    clap their hands over you;
For who has not been overwhelmed,
    steadily, by your malice?

Dirge over the city—3:18-19

18   The locusts are forgotten as the concluding verses sing a dirge over the fallen city. Addressing the city or its king (some regard the word "king" as a gloss), the poet in a glimpse of the future evokes how its leaders (frequently called "shepherds" in the Bible) now sleep the sleep of death, and its people, like sheep without a shepherd, are dispersed.

Jer 3:15;
Ez 37:24
1 K 22:17;
Mt 9:36

19   Though occasionally used of individuals, the word "wound" in the prophets usually refers to the collapse of states. The joy of neighboring nations, already suggested in 3:7, now heightens to applause. The theological justification given for this joy in the last line is probably an inspired addition from a date later than Nahum. Poetically it is anti-climactic; but it does reflect the reason why the book of Nahum was treasured in Jewish tradition. It proclaims not only an historical triumph but a theological message of great importance.

Amos 6:6;
Is 30:26

Is 55:12
Ex 25:6

THE BOOK OF HABAKKUK

Introduction

The historical problem

Hardly any book of the Old Testament has given rise to more divergent views as to the precise date of its appearance than Habakkuk (also spelt *Habacuc* in some Catholic editions of the Bible). Even at the risk of confusing the reader, some exposure to these views is necessary.

The only external evidence for dating Habakkuk is the fact that in the Jewish collection the book was included among the Prophets; and internal evidence is far from homogeneous. As our first clue we may take the mention of the Chaldeans in 1:6 as the instrument of imminent divine correction. The validity of this clue is questioned by Duhm, while C. C. Torrey maintains that the word *Kittim* (Greeks) originally stood where the Hebrew text reads *Chaldeans* (Babylonians). Thus they would place the composition in the Greek period, about 331 B.C.

Scholars generally have not accepted this thesis; a much earlier date is preferred, the word Chaldeans is accepted as authentic, and composition is placed well before the fall of Jerusalem in 587. But there is little agreement as to the precise time prior to that date. In S.R. Driver's long-respected view, Habakkuk is a collection of materials uttered over a considerable period of time and reflecting different circumstances — including oracles pronounced after the Babylonians routed the Egyptians at Carchemish in 605 B.C., through the domestic troubles of Jehoiakim's reign, down to a time near the fall of Jerusalem. Such a "collection" theory helps explain the unevenness apparent in the text. In recent years, however, with an increased understanding of the role of cult in the prophetic utterances, some writers have suggested that the liturgical purpose, already long admitted for chapter 3, is to be extended to the first two chapters. P. Humbert in 1944 proposed that Habakkuk was a cultic prophet who received his revelation in the temple and wrote the whole book as the score for a liturgical rite. The date he set was 602-601 B.C., after Carchemish and during the reign of Jehoiakim. J.H. Eaton has recently (1961) accepted the cultic explanation but pushed the date for some sections further back to the time when the rising Babylonian kingdom had not yet become a real threat to the Assyrian empire, even before 625 B.C. See the commentary on 1:6 for further details.

The point of view adopted in this commentary is the cultic one, but with the modification which seems to be imposed by the varied historical circumstances the work envisages, namely, that it was written either by a single author over a period of several years, or better by an editor who incorporated earlier traditional elements into a fresh liturgical presentation. Thus the very book of Habakkuk itself would be a brilliant illustration of the Jewish liturgical practice of "re-reading" previous texts and supplementing them with contemporary compositions. Obviously the person of Habakkuk must stand behind the substance of the book, or there would be no reason why he should be credited with it.

The message

Enigmatic as the historical question as to the date of composition may still appear, the basic theology of Habakkuk creates no problem. Long before the Wisdom writers, this prophet dared question God's justice on the international level: Why do the wicked flourish and just suffer? In a first oracle he states that a vindicator was coming in another political power rising on the horizon — the Chaldeans (1:5-11). But the answer was insufficient; at least the turn of events eventually proved it so, with the new power being as bad as the first, perhaps worse. The prophet presses his complaint and sharpens his arguments: God has revealed himself as a holy God (1:12). This means not only his transcendence—which Habakkuk implies in nature's convulsions at Yahweh's effortless glance (3:6)—but his moral responsibility: he has pure eyes (1:13), and this does not mean that he refuses to see evil, but that, having seen it, he cannot condone it. Moreover, he is a living God (1:12), and inaction would be a real "death of God." It is not only Judah but other nations as well who suffer (1:17). Why?

Then the prophet waits—the revelation of the mystery of God's dealings with man cannot be forced. The final answer, more profound than the first, is simply God's word, without further guarantee. "The just man, by his fidelity, will live" (2:4). Fidelity to Yahweh will, despite all appearances to the contrary, bring the fullness of life. The oracle climaxes there and ends. It must have brought little immediate consolation to those who expected the promise of immediate defeat of the oppressor. But it opened the way to a more universal answer to the problem of the suffering of the just and projected Israel's thought to a future restoration. In the New Testament Paul will use it to establish his doctrine that by faith the just man enters the fullness of life, the resurrection (Rm 1:17; Gal 3:11). The counterpart of this positive doctrine is that evil will work its own undoing (2:4a, 6b-8), and on the international level, the nation that isolates itself and feeds off others is doomed to ultimate collapse (2:9-11). The vision of cities built by bloodshed whets the prophet's yearning and leads him to prophesy the day when God's perfect kingdom will be established on earth (2:14). Habakkuk's vision is not only international but cosmic; yet his theophany (3:3-11) is historicized in God's intervention to save his people (3:12-18). The word *save* appears three times in the final verses of the closing canticle (3:8, 13, 18), and indicates exactly the same faith affirmed in 2:4, namely, though death itself visit land and people, the just man will somehow, in spite of all, live because of his faith in a God who saves.

Habakkuk and Qumran

Among the scrolls found in the first cave at Qumran was a commentary on Habakkuk. As in a similar commentary on Nahum, the work applies the prophecy to contemporary persons and events. The Chaldeans of 1:6 are, according to the scroll, the *Kittim*, a code word for Seleucid Greeks or perhaps the Romans, who, like the Chaldeans of old, invaded Palestine. The commentary covers only the first two chapters of Habakkuk. Antedating the Massoretic text by centuries, the ancient scroll has proved of value in correcting the readings at more than one point. The commentator's understanding of faith in 2:4 is especially significant as background for the New Testament interpretation of the passage. See below in commentary.

Outline of the Book of Habakkuk

1:1		Title
1:1–2:4	Part One:	THE DIALOGUE WITH GOD
1:2-4		First lament
1:5-11		Response
1:12-17		Second lament
2:1		The watch for Yahweh's answer
2:2-3		Yahweh's directions
2:4		Yahweh's response
2:5-20	Part Two:	CURSES UPON THE OPPRESSOR
2:5-6a		Prelude
2:6b-20		Five woes
3:1-19	Part Three:	CANTICLE FOR YAHWEH'S VICTORY
3:2		Prelude
3:3-11		Storm theophany
3:12-15		Historical meaning
3:16-19		Reaction of faith

THE BOOK OF HABAKKUK

Text and Commentary

1 The oracle which Habacuc the prophet
received in vision.
²How long, O Lord? I cry for help
but you do not listen!
I cry out to you, "Violence!"
but you do not intervene.

The title is probably a later editorial addition. The name
Habakkuk seems to have no special significance. It may be related to the Akkadian *habaququ* or *hambaququ*, the name of
a plant and fruit tree. The account of Habakkuk's "hair-lift"
trip to nourish Daniel in the lion's den is of a different literary
genre, and we do not even know if the author of Daniel was
thinking of Habakkuk, the author of this book. From the contents and form of the book, the case is quite strong for iden-
tifying Habakkuk as a cult prophet who exercised his office in
the temple.

Dn
14:33-39

I. THE DIALOGUE WITH GOD
Hb 1:2—2:4

First lament—1:2-4

The first part of Habakkuk is a dialogue with God. The prophet, speaking for the community, utters two complaints; to each
of these Yahweh answers in an oracle. In the first the prophet
dares (in what may be called the first instance in Hebrew
literature) to call God to account for his way of governing
the world, viz., for his "permission of evil" as we would
say today. If the form is that of a "collective complaint," in
which the sentiments of a group are expressed by a leader in
the name of all and couched in traditional terms, then the
whole lament could be understood of some foreign enemy,
even though the words "law" and "judgment" are traditional
terms for internal strife. Other scholars point precisely to
these terms as indicating that the whole section (2-4) refers
to the domestic situation in Judah, such as was doubtless
the case prior to the battle of Carchemish in 605 B.C. At any

> ³Why do you let me see ruin;
>   why must I look at misery?
> Destruction and violence are before me;
>   there is strife, and clamorous discord.
> ⁴This is why the law is benumbed,
>   and judgment is never rendered:
> Because the wicked circumvent the just;
>   this is why judgment comes forth perverted.
> ⁵Look over the nations and see,
>   and be utterly amazed!
> For a work is being done in your days
>   that you would not have believed, were it told.
> ⁶For see, I am raising up Chaldea,
>   that bitter and unruly people,

rate, the prophet gives vent to his dismay that a just God could allow such trouble; a lament of this type will reoccur in Ps 22 and be repeated by Jesus on the Cross. It is not a cry of despair but of dismay and urgency, and the God who apparently does not hear is precisely the one addressed; for the prophet knows that apart from God there is no help at all.

Response—1:5-11

The answer now comes as an oracle of Yahweh. It is addressed to a mixed audience, probably first to the temple prophets and later to assembled worshippers. They are invited to look to the theater of international events and witness an act of God so astounding that most people simply will not believe it. The text implies that the message is an instance of genuine prophetic insight and not merely something which any astute political observer of the day might plausibly predict. The rise of the Chaldeans was no mere accident; they would serve as an instrument of God's justice. Chaldea was a province of southern Babylonia. Originally from the west coast of the Persian Gulf, the Chaldeans had migrated into southern Mesopotamia during the early centuries of the first millenium B.C. and fell victim to the Assyrian yoke. Under Nabopolassar the Chaldeans finally secured the independence of Babylonia in 626 B.C. and went on to destroy the Assyrian capital of Nineveh in 612. But even before Nabopolassar, the Babylonians had been a growing threat to the Assyrian empire, and there is no sound reason why the perspective of the present passage should not antedate 626. The following reasons support such a view: (1) The vision is obviously meant to be

Is 53:1

> That marches the breadth of the land
>   to take dwellings not his own.
> 7Terrible and dreadful is he,
>   from himself derive his law and his majesty.
> 8Swifter than leopards are his horses,
>   and keener than wolves at evening.
> His horses prance,
>   his horsemen come from afar:
> They fly like the eagle hastening to devour;
> 9 each comes for the rapine,
> Their combined onset is that of a stormwind
>   that heaps up captives like sand.

a prediction; the actual sequence and character of events after 625 does not correspond to the prophecy and suggests that the latter was a visionary description in mythological terms of what was to come. (2) The prophet expects his oracle to be met with incredulity (1:5), which would hardly have been the case were there a widespread and reasonable hope that Assyria would fall to the Chaldeans. (3) After 625 the Assyrian empire deteriorated so rapidly that it could hardly have been causing the trouble which dismayed Habakkuk; rather Assyria appears as an international tyrant with a long record. Neither do the Egyptians nor Jehoiakim measure up to his description. Consequently, internal evidence suggests dating this oracle quite early, at a time when no one, or not more than a few, would have identified Chaldea as holding the key to the future. When the prophecy came true, its divine origin was felt to be authenticated, and this accounted for its preservation in Israelite tradition. There must, after all, be some explanation why King Josiah and many Judahites were so ready to ally themselves, at great risk, with the Chaldaens. A prophecy such as this one could have bolstered an otherwise uncertain political hope.

The terms Habakkuk used to describe the Chaldeans and their military tactics are traditional ones bordering on the mythological, and not far from apocalyptic. Habakkuk is no sympathizer with the morality or religiosity of the Chaldeans. Deriving his *mišpat* (judgment, law) as well as his awesome might from his own self-reliance rather than from Yahweh, the Chaldean is the incarnation of pride, and a distant forerunner of that apocalyptic adversary depicted in Daniel and later in the New Testament.

Is
14:12-14
Dn 11:36f

The horses, swift, impatient, possessed by the drive of the

> 10He scoffs at kings,
>   and princes are his laughingstock;
> He laughs at any fortress,
>   heaps up a ramp, and conquers it.
> 11Then he veers like the wind and is gone —
>   this culprit who makes his own strength his god!
> 12Are you not from eternity, O Lord,
>   my holy God, immortal?
> O Lord, you have marked him for judgment,
>   O Rock, you have set him up for punishment!
> 13Too pure are your eyes to look upon evil,
>   and the sight of misery you cannot endure.

wolf at evening in hunt for prey, rush in with the suddenness
9 of the swooping eagle. The rapid marshalling of scenes cul-
minates in that of the sandstorm: in a like fashion will
10-11 the Chaldean pile up captives. After the city is conquered, the
Chaldean, like the Assyrian, will set up a local puppet who
will guarantee tribute and then he will be gone, with the swift-
ness of the wind. The translation of the final verse of this
oracle is uncertain. The expression "culprit" (or "guilty men",
RSV) is the reading of the MT, but the Qumran scroll of Habakkuk has a different reading which suggests simply "and
this one makes his strength his god."

Jer 5:6
Zeph 3:3

Second lament—1:12-17

The answer to the first complaint was either insufficient, or,
more probably, the historical situation at a later period had
worsened. At any rate this second lament is longer, more specific and more impassioned than the first. Most critics take
it as referring to the Chaldeans who are now persecuting the
community.

12   Of two things the prophet is convinced: God is holy, God
is living. "Immortal" (lit. "you die not") means, in Hebrew
thought, not eternity but a living and active presence. God is
not dead! (The second half of v. 12 anticipates an answer
and is probably a later intrusion into the original text.)
13 Sharpening what he has just said, the prophet describes
God's holiness in the beautiful image of pure eyes — too
pure to look upon (i.e., condone) evil or to remain unmoved
at the misery of his chosen ones. But this credo of the Israel-
14-15 ite is being challenged by his daily experience. God is silent in
the presence of evident evil, unmoved at misery. It is the
mystery of God's providence that is causing anguish here:

> Why, then, do you gaze on the faithless in silence
>   while the wicked man devours
>   one more just than himself?
> 14You have made man like the fish of the sea,
>   like creeping things without a master.
> 15He brings them all up with his hook,
>   he hauls them away with his net,
> He gathers them in his seine;
>   and so he rejoices and exults.
> 16Therefore he sacrifices to his net,
>   and burns incense to his seine;
> For thanks to them his portion is generous,
>   and his repast sumptuous.
> 17Shall he, then, keep on brandishing his sword
>   to slay peoples without mercy?

for it seems that the more righteous (the Israelites) are treated no better than the fish to which God pays no attention, leaving them to the accidents of nature. The lower animals may have no master, but the people certainly do, and it is Yahweh himself! Why then are his people treated like fish, hooked and seined and carried away into captivity — an allusion probably to the deportations practiced by the Babylonians, like the Assyrians before them. An Assyrian re-

16 lief shows Esarhaddon holding the kings of Sidon and Ethiopia on a leash, with a ring through their lips. The image of sacrificing to the net simply carries on the image, with the implied complaint that Yahweh is allowing this idolatrous business to continue. The reference may be to a rite involving a cultic veneration of the weapons of war. Herodotus says the Scythians made an annual sacrifice to a sword

17 as an image of their god of war (*History* IV, 62). It is not only his elect but other nations who endure this brutality. How can the holy and living God permit it to go on?

The watch for Yahweh's answer—2:1

1   To stress its greater importance, a greater solemnity introduces the answer to this second lament. The answer to a prophetic lament was not to be had at will; ever since the revelation that Yahweh is "he who (really) is," Israel knew   Ex 3:14
that her God was not in a box, to be reached by turning a key. Jeremiah prayed for ten days before he received an answer   Jer 42:4, 7
for the army leaders. The psalms often speak of waiting, even   Ps 5:3
until the dawn, for an answer to prayer.

2 I will stand at my guard post,
    and station myself upon the rampart,
And keep watch to see what he will say to me,
    and what answer he will give to my complaint.
2Then the Lord answered me and said:
    Write down the vision
Clearly upon the tablets,
    so that one can read it readily.
3For the vision still has its time,
    presses on to fulfillment, and will not disappoint;
If it delays, wait for it,
    it will surely come, it will not be late.
4The rash man has no integrity;
    but the just man, because of his faith, shall live.
5Wealth, too, is treacherous:
    the proud, unstable man —

The prophets were often depicted as watchmen. What we have here are some technical terms which reflect a cultic practice by the temple prophets for receiving an oracle. The direct speech may itself have been part of the liturgical enactment of the prophet's vigil.

Is 21:6ff;
56:10
Is 50:4f
2 Chr 7:6

Yahweh's direction—2:2-3

Suspense is heightened as the heart of the oracle is delayed further by the directions the prophet receives from the Lord. Since most prophecy was communicated orally, a special command to write it down accentuates its importance. "That one can read it readily" is literally, "so that he may run who reads it." The tablets are probably of wood or stone; and the message is to be written like a sign in large letters and posted at some conspicuous spot in the temple. The fulfillment of the vision is not to take place immediately, but the inscription will be there to sustain those who await its promise.

3

Yahweh's response—2:4

The message which really forms the heart of Habakkuk's prophecy is now revealed. Like many other prophetic oracles, it is a pronouncement both of judgment and salvation. The first member of the verse is difficult to translate. The Hebrew says literally, "Behold, his soul within him is puffed up, not right." Contrasted with the second member, the sense becomes clear enough: the oppressor, puffed up as he is with pride and injustice, already has within him the seeds of his own destruction, and time will inevitably reap its toll. The

He who opens wide his throat like the nether world,
  and is insatiable as death,
Who gathers to himself all the nations,
  and rallies to himself all the peoples —
⁶Shall not all these take up a taunt against him,
  satire and epigrams about him, to say:
Woe to him who stores up what is not his:
  how long can it last!
  he loads himself down with debts.
⁷Shall not your creditors rise suddenly?

Qumran commentator perceived this sense: "Interpreted, this means that (the wicked) shall double their guilt upon themselves (and it shall not be forgiven) when they are judged." On the contrary, the just man in his fidelity will live. The just man is he who is right in his relations with God and his fellow man. Here is the ideal of moral and religious perfection of both Old and New Testaments. That which makes man just is his *'emunah*, his faith, in the sense of fidelity, loyal, trusting and persevering attachment to Yahweh manifested in the observance of his covenant. What is stressed here, in the context of long-suffering, is an underlying constancy rooted in trust that God will fulfill his promises; of this spirit Abraham was the supreme example: "Abraham *believed* the Lord, who credited the act to him as justice." In our present text, the final words, "he shall live," occupy the place of honor; thereby the statement obtains the emphatic sense of "he will have the fullness of life." To live in this sense is not merely to exist but to enter into the promises of God. The three Hebrew words which form this expression (*ṣadiq b*ᵉ *'emunatho yihyeh*) are the quintessence of both the Old and the New Testaments. Against all odds, the just man (*ṣaddiq*) rebounded with a credo that, no matter what life presently looked like, fidelity to Yahweh would in the end bring life in all its fullness. The term "life" remained open-ended. The Servant of Yahweh, persevering in trust and fidelity through death, will "see the light in fullness of days." By the time the Book of Daniel was written, under oppression quite similar to that described by Habakkuk, the fullness of life had come to mean "eternal life" and final resurrection of the just. In this sense the New Testament promises eternal life to him who believes. Belief there takes on the added dimension of acceptance of the act of God in Christ. This further meaning of the personal acceptance of God's envoy was prepared for by

Gn 15:6
Rm 4:3

Is 53:11

Dn 12:2f
Jn 3:15,
36; 6:40

Shall not they who make you tremble awake?
  You shall become their spoil!
8Because you despoiled many peoples
  all the rest of the nations shall despoil you;
 Because of men's blood shed,
   and violence done to the land,
  to the city and to all who dwell in it.
9Woe to him who pursues evil gain for his household,
  setting his nest on high
   to escape the reach of misfortune!

the Qumran community's understanding of our Habakkuk
text. The commentary reads: "Interpreted, this concerns all
those who observe the Law in the house of Judah, whom God
will deliver from the house of judgment because of their suffering and because of their faith in the Teacher of Righteous-
ness." Paul makes use of Hb 2:4 twice; and in the definition
of the Gospel he gives in Romans it is obvious that "life" is
identical with "salvation." "I am not ashamed of the gospel,
for it is the power of God leading to salvation for everyone
who believes. . . As it is written, 'He who is just will live
because of his faith.'"

Gal 3:11
Rm 1:16f

II. CURSES UPON THE OPPRESSOR
Hb 2:5-20

This section elaborates upon the misery and misfortunes
which the first line of the oracle promised for the oppressor.
It is comprised of a prelude followed by five "woes" hurled at
the unjust.

Prelude—2:5-6a

"Wealth" is a fitting word to characterize the Chaldeans. All
the nations who have been swallowed up by Babylon's insatiable greed now turn against her; they voice their scorn in the
form of satire (mašal, mockery in figurative language) and
epigram (melișah, a riddle requiring interpretation). Let him
whom the shoe fits wear it!

Five woes—2:6b-20

A crescendo of five curses builds to a climax in 19-20. Without the historical context known to Habakkuk's listeners, we
have great difficulty in determining to whom each of these
curses applies. Most commentators settle for the Chaldeans

10You have devised shame for your household,
    cutting off many peoples, forfeiting your own life:
11For the stone in the wall shall cry out,
    and the beam in the woodwork shall answer it!
12Woe to him who builds a city by bloodshed,
    and establishes a town by wickedness!
13Is not this from the Lord of hosts:
    people toil for the flames,
    and nations grow weary for nought!
14But the earth shall be filled
    with the knowledge of the Lord's glory
    as water covers the sea.
15Woe to you who give your neighbors
    a flood of your wrath to drink,
    and make them drunk, till their nakedness is seen!

(some, the Assyrians). Others would see them directed to the
Judean king who had put his trust in the nations, specifically Egypt. The latter interpretation, plausible for certain
elements, is difficult to sustain for the entire series of woes.

6b-8 The first woe attacks the greed of the conquerer. An ironic
reversal: the conqueror appears to be the creditor, but he is
really the debtor. It is the application on the international scene
of the law of talion, the constant prophetic theme that evil   Ex 21:25
will eventually be its own undoing.

9-11 More grievous is the crime depicted in the second woe.
It is one thing to be avaricious; it is another to use ill-
gotten goods to seal oneself off from the misfortune of others.
The king (or the people he represents) has built a palace
as an eagle builds its nest far above the strife of the common world. He has, temporarily at least, succeeded in cutting
off many nations and establishing himself in self-sufficiency.
To no avail. To do so is to forfeit one's own life. The very
stones and woodwork cry out in alternating execration of his   Lk 19:40
self-imposed isolation. It is indeed an unusual sense of international justice and solidarity which the prophet here reveals,
two and a half millenia before *Pacem in Terris* and *Populorum
Progressio*. Though the description closely resembles Jeremiah's philippic on Jehoiakim, the detail about cutting off   Jer
many peoples could only apply to international conduct and   22:13-17
is more easily applicable to a foreign oppressor.

12-14 The third woe is directed against rule by violence. It has   Mi 3:10;
several parallels in prophetic literature, and the suggestion has   Jer 51:58;
been made that it is a later composite by a scribe who com-   Is 11:9
bined well known texts. In the light of what is now known about

16You are filled with shame instead of glory;
   drink, you too, and stagger!
On you shall revert the cup from the Lord's right hand,
   and utter shame on your glory.
17For the violence done to Lebanon shall cover you,
   and the destruction of the beasts shall terrify you; ·
Because of men's blood shed,
   and violence done to the land,
   to the city and to all who dwell in it.
19Woe to him who says to wood, "Awake!"
   to dumb stone, "Arise!"
Can such a thing give oracles?
See, it is overlaid with gold and silver,
   but there is no life breath in it.

oral prophetic tradition, such an interpretation is wholly un-
necessary. It may reflect traditional prophetic themes which
were current in the temple liturgy. After setting forth the futil-
ity of building by violence, the prophet looks forward to the
ideal kingdom which God will one day bring into existence.

15-17 The law of retribution is applied in the fourth woe. The
oppressor (Assyria or Babylonia, it makes no difference), had
been sweeping over the nations, making them reel as if drunk,
leaving them, like Noah, open to nakedness, shame and abuse.
In a sense the conqueror had been the instrument of pouring
out the cup of God's wrath. But now in his turn, the con-   Ob 16;
queror is made to drink the same cup. Where our version on   Is 51:17
the basis of the Septuagint reads, "Drink, you too, and stagger," most versions follow the Massoretic text, "Drink, you
17 too, and show yourself uncircumcised." Inscriptions of both the
Assyrians and the Babylonians attest to the cutting down of
the timber of Lebanon. The prophets considered the reck-   Is 37:24;
less exploitation of these magnificent forests and the killing of   14:8
beasts found there a particular sign of the wickedness of the
conqueror; that crime, Habakkuk says, will now rebound upon him. Another example of the "violence to the land" was
given by Sennacherib when in 689 he plowed up the city of
Babylon and cast a symbolic portion of its soil into the river.

18-20 Verses 18 and 19 render better sense if, as in done in the
CV, their order is reversed and the "woe" comes first.
This final curse is upon idolatry, in language closely resem-   Is 41:6f;
bling that of Second Isaiah. The contrast between the dynamic   44:9-20;
power of the living God and the lifeless (breathless, without   Jer 10:2-9

18Of what avail is the carved image,
    that its maker should carve it?
Or the molten image and lying oracle,
    that its very maker should trust in it,
    and make dumb idols?
20But the Lord is in his holy temple;
    silence before him, all the earth!

Prayer of Habacuc, the prophet. To a plaintive tune.

3 O Lord, I have heard your renown,
    and feared, O Lord, your work.
2In the course of the years revive it,
    in the course of the years make it known;
    in your wrath remember compassion!

ruah), speechless character of the gold-covered idol could
hardly be made more striking.

20   The passage concludes with the serene affirmation of
Israelite faith: God is in his holy temple. The prophet is thinking of God's temple of heaven, of which the temple in Jerusalem was considered the counterpart. He is stirring there, about
to intervene. The prophet calls for silence—a liturgical rubric   Zeph 1:7
associated with temple worship is now extended to the   Zech 2:13
entire earth. Besides making a fitting conclusion to all that
preceded, the line is a perfect preparation for the theophany
about to take place in the next chapter.

III. THE CANTICLE FOR YAHWEH'S VICTORY
Hb 3:1-19

This magnificent hymn differs in form from the preceding,
is provided with liturgical rubrics, and lacks any specific historical reference. These elements make it difficult to pin-point
the occasion of its composition, and many critics opt for the
postexilic period. However, the psalm provides a fine climax
to the preceding chapters, and there is greater probability that
Habakkuk himself composed the hymn as a liturgical crown
for his work. The special title in v. 1 would have arisen when
the psalm was later used separately.

The best occasion suggested for the psalm's liturgical usage
is the Autumn Festival, the time of prayer for the winter
rains to renew the parched earth; on such feasts it was in
order to add a supplication for deliverance from political
enemies. The idea of the death of nature appears in this
hymn (v. 17), as well as God's magnificent coming in a
rainstorm (9f). Some of the coloring may be of the same
hue as found in Babylonian creation myths or Canaanite

> ³God comes from Theman,
>   the Holy One from Mount Pharan.
> Covered are the heavens with his glory,
>   and with his praise the earth is filled.
> ⁴His splendor spreads like the light;
>   rays shine forth from beside him,
>   where his power is concealed.
> ⁵Before him goes pestilence,
>   and the plague follows in his steps.
> ⁶He pauses to survey the earth;
>   his look makes the nations tremble.
> The eternal mountains are shattered,

(Ugaritic) epics on Baal's triumph over the primordial sea; **Is 51:9f**
but actually, our prophet by combining motifs from Genesis
and Exodus sees Yahweh's intervention in nature and history
as one. The psalm echoes and expands the answers already
given to the prophet's two complaints of 1:2-4 and 12-17.

Prelude—3:2

Addressing Yahweh directly, the prophet reminds him of his
great saving deeds of the past which have won him renown. **Ps 44:1-8**
"Fearing" here has the sense of awe; some versions change it
to "see." "In the course of the years" here means "in our
present time." In the outburst of divine vindication that is
about to take place, the prophet prays that a shelter may be
granted to those who trust in Yahweh. Or: may you show
your mercy to us by intervening now in our behalf.

Storm theophany—3:3-11

3 The answer to the prophet's prayer now comes in a vision;
God is no longer addressed but described, and the ancient term
Eloah is used. From the southern desert, the direction from
which the autumn winds herald the change of the season,
God comes. Teman and Paran, both in Edom, are used here
in a theophany context as the equivalent of Sinai; stressed **Dt 33:2**
is the breadth of the theophany — God's rays shine from the
heights of Paran west of the Arabah to those of Teman to
4 the east. All creation is filled with his glory. Like the sun
rising and sending forth shafts of light is God's coming. "And
there is hidden his power." Usually, the image of the cloud is **Ex 20:21;**
used as the "covering" of the glory of God; but here light itself **13:21**
is depicted as his garment; sunlight both reveals and conceals
his power, inasmuch as it is a mere earthly manifestation of **Ps 104:2**
him who dwells in light inaccessible. **1 Tim 6:16**

> the age-old hills bow low
>   along his ancient ways.
> 7I see the tents of Chusan collapse;
>   trembling are the pavilions of the land of Madian.
> 8Is your anger against the streams, O Lord?
>   Is your wrath against the streams,
>   your rage against the sea,
> That you drive the steeds
>   of your victorious chariot?
> 9Bared and ready is your bow,
>   filled with arrows is your quiver.
> Into streams you split the earth;
> 10   at sight of you the mountains tremble.
> A torrent of rain descends;
>   the ocean gives forth its roar.
> The sun forgets to rise,

5   Before him, like a shield-bearer goes pestilence, behind him like a servant, fever (literally, burning heat) — perhaps an allusion to the searing sirocco which precedes the rainstorm. Near Eastern peoples often thought of pestilence or a deadly wind as a demon accompanying a god — as Marduk was accompanied when he did battle with Tiamat: "An Evil Wind, which followed behind, he let loose in her face" (ANET 66).

6   The Lord's effortless glance upon the earth contrasts with its cataclysmic effects. "Along his ancient ways" is taken by our version as applying to the hills, the oldest and firmest part of the earth. It is more in keeping with the context to translate these words as a substantive clause: "His are ways of the olden time," i.e., he now advances just as he did in the time of Sinai, when the mountains trembled at his appearance and neighboring nations were thrown into fear and despair. The nomad

7   tents of Midian and Cushan (seemingly an ancient name for the same region) flutter and collapse under the driving wind of Yahweh.

8-10   Heightening the poetic intensity, the prophet addresses Yahweh himself. The storm theophany is here. To the spectator, it seems indeed like a battle of waves lashing up to the heavens, met there by thunderbolts. Genesis had depicted God's creative activity in terms of harnessing the primeval watery chaos, his wrath in terms of unleashing it; here one may recall the dividing of the Red Sea or of the Jordan but on a grander scale. "Victorious chariot" is literally, "your chariots of salvation," a preparation for v. 13. God is depicted as a cosmic chariot-driver bringing salvation to his people.

Jb 20:4;
Ps 90:2

Jg 5:5
Ex
15:14-16

Gn 1:2ff

Gn 7:11

11   the moon remains in its shelter,
   At the light of your flying arrows,
      at the gleam of your flashing spear.
12In wrath you bestride the earth,
   in fury you trample the nations.
13You come forth to save your people,
   to save your anointed one.
 You crush the heads of the wicked,
   you lay bare their bases at the neck.
14You pierce with your shafts the heads of their princes
   whose boast would be of devouring
   the wretched in their lair.
15You tread the sea with your steeds
   amid the churning of the deep waters.
16I hear, and my body trembles;
   at the sound, my lips quiver.

God's bow is bared and his arrows, lightning-bolts, are ready. *Dt 32:23*
An earthquake splits the earth and the waters of the deep are *Gn 7:11*
loosed, to be joined by the waters from the heavens.

   All is darkness save for the arrows and the spear of Yahweh.
The clouds have obscured the sun, moon, and stars, but the
author depicts them as frightened back to their "dwelling- *Ps 77:18*
places" by the brilliant display of God's lightning.

Historical meaning—3:12-15

   The historical realization of the cosmic theophany is now explained. It is a saving intervention in favor of Yahweh's people *Is 53:1-6*
and of the king who is his anointed. There is no hint as to
which king is envisioned; liturgical re-use no doubt made application to the contemporary king, while during and after the
exile men's minds turned to the Messiah. Vv. 13b and 14 resemble the description of Marduk's splitting the skull of
Tiamat (ANET 67). V. 15 concludes the theophany with references again to the storm at sea.

Reaction of faith—3:16-19

16   The prophet now meditates on what he has seen. His first re-
      action is fright at what is about to come to pass. But it will
      be upon enemies that the "day of distress" will fall. "Who
      attack us" indicates the psalm was composed in a period of
17-18 national crisis. Yet no matter how much national life under
      such oppression may present the aspect of a land withered
      from drought, the prophet renews his faith in an out-
      burst of joy in the Lord, for he knows him to be a *saving* God.

> Decay invades my bones,
>> my legs tremble beneath me.
> I await the day of distress
>> that will come upon the people who attack us.
> 17For though the fig tree blossom not
>> nor fruit be on the vines,
> Though the yield of the olive fail
>> and the terraces produce no nourishment,
> Though the flocks disappear from the fold
>> and there be no herd in the stalls,
> 18Yet will I rejoice in the Lord
>> and exult in my saving God.
> 19God, my Lord, is my strength;
>> he makes my feet swift as those of hinds
>> and enables me to go upon the heights.

And finally, in words that are the traditional expression of the king's trust in God, the prophet sings of Yahweh as his strength and as the source of his sprightliness resembling the doe that leaps with gracious ease to the mountain heights. Ps 18:33

The exact meaning of the final rubric, directed to the "leader," is not clear. It is precious, nevertheless, as it is a final indication of the continual re-use of this salvation psalm by God's people as they faced persecution and death and defied both in the name of Yahweh, the God who through death comes to save, and who promised that the just man by his fidelity will see life to the full. Hb 2:4

THE BOOK OF LAMENTATIONS

Introduction

Authorship and date

Lamentations is found in the third and final part of the Hebrew Bible, the part known as the "Writings." Here in a subsection entitled "Megilloth" or "Rolls", Lamentations occupies a position preceded by the Song of Songs and Ruth, and followed by Ecclesiastes and Esther. Since about the year 70 A.D., Lamentations has been used in orthodox Jewry on the ninth of Ab to commemorate the fall of the temple, but already during the exile and doubtless on other occasions after the return, it was sung by a people saddened over the destruction of Jerusalem.

In the Septuagint versions (except for a few manuscripts, notably Codex Vaticanus) and in the Vulgate, Lamentations appears immediately after Jeremiah and bears the title, "Lamentations of Jeremiah." This long tradition accrediting to Jeremiah the authorship Lamentations is based on 2 Chr 35:25: "Jeremiah composed a lament for Josiah which all the singing men and singing women still recite today when they lament for Josiah; this has become a custom in Israel; the dirges are recorded in the Lamentations." Traces of lamentation for Josiah are found in Jer 22:10, 15, 18 and perhaps the Chronicler assumed some references to Josiah in the Lamentations (as for example 2:1-3). At any rate, the Targum, followed by all the early commentators, interpreted 4:20 as referring to Josiah, and hence it is easy to see how the whole book came to be attributed to Jeremiah. The weight of this evidence becomes scant when it is recalled that Lamentations is devoted exclusively to the fall of Jerusalem, and 4:20 obviously refers to Zedekiah. But at this very point the Septuagint offers a final testimony to the authorhip of Jeremiah. At the head of the text it states: "And it came to pass, after Israel was taken captive and Jerusalem laid waste, that Jeremiah sat weeping and lamented with this lamentation over Jerusalem and said. . . ." The Syriac, Old Latin and Vuigate have the same heading, and chances are that it reflects a more ancient Hebrew text.

However, there are serious difficulties in admitting Jeremiah as author. The prophet of Anatoth could hardly have said that the voice of prophecy is dead (Lam 2:19). He who had fulminated against relying on Egypt for aid (Jer 37:5-10) could hardly have aligned himself with those who did (Lam 4:17). He who was so certain of the fate of Zedekiah (Jer 37:17-20) could hardly have been so dismayed when his own prophecy was fulfilled (Lam 4:20). Moreover, it is hard to see how Jeremiah, so given to passionate outbursts, could have disciplined himself to the artificial literary scheme followed in these poems. There is also a significant difference in vocabulary. To these data of internal criticism comes the additional fact that the collection of the "Writings" was the last to be accepted into the canon of the Hebrew scriptures. Had Lamentations been associated with Jeremiah from the earliest hour, it would surely have been incorporated with the prophetical works as having the authority of Jeremiah himself. The tradition linking the work with him is therefore late. Certain Greek manuscripts, including the Codex Vaticanus, have only the title "Lamentations" without mention of Jeremiah, and this has all the probability of being a rendering of the original Hebrew, as it would be otherwise difficult to explain the omission of such an important personage as their author.

If Jeremiah is excluded as author, what clues are there to indicate who wrote the book and when? The graphic descriptions of the miseries during and following the fall of Jerusalem, particularly in the second and fourth lamentation, argue strongly for composition shortly after the events, when the emotional impact of the tragedy was still fresh. Jeremiah 41:5 indicates that the liturgy continued to be celebrated on the temple site after its destruction. Since the Lamentations were obviously composed with a view to liturgical recitation, evidence would point to some anonymous poet in Palestine shortly after 587 BC. This certainly is valid for the second and fourth Lamentations and there is no serious reason for denying the first lament to the same author, though its description of the fall itself is less vivid and more concerned with the effects upon the city. The fifth may be of later date, but not much later, since there is no hint of any immediate restoration.

The third Lamentation occupies the central position in the book and apparently was intended by the author or at least by the final editor to be central likewise in importance. It is a much more artificial acrostic than the others and offers a more profound interpretation of the meaning of suffering. These and other elements, notably the appearance of *Elyon* as a title for God (3:35, 38), lead many authors to place the composition after the exile. But the grounds for such late dating are shaky indeed, based as they are merely on the fact that ch. 3 has the form of a personal lament and lacks the vivid details of the other poems. The argument from the title Elyon is circuitous, and may now be totally invalidated by growing evidence that there was a pre-Israelite cult of Elyon at Jerusalem. At any rate, there is no need to deny the composition of any of the first four poems to the same author. And even if this is done, the intention of the final editor, which is obvious upon analysis, suffices as a clue to the book's inspired meaning.

Structure and form

The book of Lamentations is a studied artistic masterpiece. The poetic rhythm that prevails throughout is the so-called *Qinah* or lament meter, in which the first *stich* (or half-line) has three accents, and the second, two. Even so, this basic rhythm is frequently varied, and in the final lament, it is the 3/3 meter that prevails.

More significant, however, is the acrostic form. The beginning letter of each verse follows the order of the Hebrew alphabet, from *Aleph* to *Tau*. It is only in Lamentations that the pattern is carried to such lengths — 266 lines, 90 lines longer than its nearest rival, psalm 119. Obviously, the acrostic form facilitates memorization, but it imposes considerable limitations on the spontaneity of the author. Why, then, did an author so engulfed by tragedy choose to limit his expression by this literary form? Several explanations have been offered. The most obvious one is that already mentioned, as an aid to memorization. If the poems were composed separately for different days of lamentation and without any intention at first to collect them, the *aide-memoire* explanation is indeed plausible. On the other hand, if they were written as a whole, the utility for memorization would be virtually nil, for how could one avoid confusing, for example, the *Beth* line in the second poem with the *Beth* line in the fourth?

The principal reason for this choice is convincingly developed by N. K. Gottwald, *Studies in the Book of Lamentations* (London: SCM Press, 1962). The listing of the entire alphabet gives a sense of completeness, of totally exhausting a subject. In the alphabet the Babylonians saw the cosmic circle. While not embracing the magical ideas associated with this view, the author of Lamentations seems to have felt as we do today, that a subject has been completely treated when it is covered "from A to Z." This sentiment underlies the Jewish use of the alphabetical form for the *widui*, lists of sins and sinners used for confessional purposes, as also such rabbinic expressions as: "Adam transgressed the whole law from *Aleph* to *Tau*" and "Abraham kept the whole law from *Aleph* to *Tau*."

Thus the primary reason for the acrostic form is to express the completeness of grief. This does not mean, however, that the emotion is entirely spent as in wild and irrational grief. Rather, the very literary discipline imposed by the form indicates restraint of emotion and insinuates a burden of meaning which goes beyond the expression of words.

The reader may at times feel that the expression of anguish is excessively repetitive. One may answer that those deeply grieved tend to say the same things over and over; but there is the more significant fact that Lamentations is not merely a catharsis of grief but also a prayer for God's mercy and intervention. Repetition thus affirms by example the value of persistence in prayer, to be recommended one day by Jesus himself (Lk 18:1-8).

Theology and significance of Lamentations

Until recently the theological significance of Lamentations has received scant attention. Most manuals and commentaries have been concerned with the question of the authorship and the integrity of the book. But within the last decade there has been renewed interest in the work, with a greater realization of its importance in the development of revelation.

For one thing, if we exclude Jeremiah, the Book of Lamentations is the first piece of literature to emerge from the ashes of the catastrophe of 587 B.C., which was the greatest crisis Israelite faith had ever faced. In the midst of a tragedy that would have led most pagan peoples to assume that their gods had been vanquished and to accept a syncretism with the gods of the conquerors, the inspired poet not only rejects this view, but he is the first to say that it was Yahweh himself who was responsible for the catastrophe, and for good reason: Judah's infidelity. Lamentations, then, is the first book to pick up the prophetic interpretation of history, which the leaders of the city had made every effort to silence, and to apply it to the fall of the city and the temple. In this, Lamentations brings important qualifications to the election theology of the Old Testament and is a stepping stone to the universalism of Second Isaiah (cf. Lam 3:37-39).

More specifically, the theology of Lamentations can be summarized in several distinct motifs, which are here elaborated separately and numbered. Numbers corresponding to these motifs are found in the margins of the commentary where the motif applies.

#1. Tragic reversal

The poet stood in a tradition which expressed grief in terms of a dramatic contrast between what once *was* and what now *is*. This contrast appears already in the funeral songs by which the Hebrews honored and mourned their dead. These songs comprised two elements:

praise for the dead, and lamentation for their passing — the contrast
often being pressed by emphasizing the most striking elements of their
past glory with their sudden, tragic demise. A striking example of this
tragic reversal is David's lament over Saul and Jonathan, beginning
with "Alas, the *glory* of Israel has been *slain* on your heights! How
the *heroes* are *fallen*!" (2 S 1:19-27). The transition from the death
of individuals to the defeat of the nation was natural and unconscious
(2 S 1:20), and with it the contrast between the present exalted state
of the enemy and Israel's misery. This motif is exploited at length by
the author of Lamentations. Once a bustling city, Jerusalem is lonely;
once a mistress, she is now a widow; once a princess, she is now a slave
(1:1); her glory has faded (1:6) and been cast from heaven to earth
(2:1). Examples become more numerous in the second lament, and
persist throughout the five lamentations.

#2. The city personified as a woman

The representation of the city as a daughter or maiden is not original
with Lamentations, but it is relatively more frequent here than in any
other book of the Old Testament, appearing no less than 17 times.
The title varies: daughter Zion (1:6; 2:1, 4, 8, 10; 2:18; 4:22),
virgin daughter Zion (2:13); daughter Judah (2:5), virgin daughter
Judah (1:15), daughter Jerusalem (2:13, 15), daughter of my people
(2:11; 4:3, 6, 10). This title of tenderness is aptly chosen to express
the poignancy of her humiliation and the disgrace of her infidelity to
Yahweh (1:19). The representation of Jerusalem as a bereaved widow
is in keeping with the theme of tragic reversal. In the ancient Orient
poverty and a social stigma were attached to widowhood (Is 1:23; 10:2;
Ez 22:7; Lv 21:14; 1 K 17:10-12; Jb 24:3, 21). The image of a desolate woman would later be chosen for the Titus memorial coin, with the
inscription, *Judaea Capta*. The poet, like the prophets before him,
but in a more conscious way, sees no inconsistency in depicting the
city as a virgin and as a mother. The terminology is thus set which
will be used in 4 Ezra, in Paul who depicts the heavenly Jerusalem as
"our mother" (Gal 4:25ff), and in the Apocalypse, where the image
of a mother and virgin-bride are both used to depict the people of
God (Apoc 12; 21).

#3. Sin

The Book of Lamentations is not merely a prolonged weeping over
lost fortunes. It is likewise a serious confession of guilt. The punishment
fits the crime and brings it into the open. To emphasize the awesome
gravity of Judah's sin, the poet twice uses the infinitive absolute (1:8,

20) and calls on a rich vocabulary running the gamut of cognate meanings but significantly avoiding the word *š^egagah*, error or sin out of inadvertence. Judah was sinning and she knew it. A comparison of our book with the Sumerian lamentation over the destruction of Ur (ANET 455-463) shows at once the preponderant emphasis placed by the Biblical poet on the moral responsibility of the people for their fate. Except for an unusual prayer for purification at the end, the Sumerian lamentation is totally given to a recitation of the woes of the city and supplications for restoration, and there is no causal relationship expressed between the sin of the people and the catastrophe. Even within the Bible itself, laments which contain a confession of sin are rare (Ps 51; 130). Basic to the poet's motivation is the conviction that forgiveness and restoration can never be imparted without a confession of sin. In fact, he is aware that Yahweh has *not* yet forgiven (3:42), and the confession of sin is aimed at winning that forgiveness. Nor is confession alone sufficient; there must be a real *turning* of self to God, repentance and conversion (5:21).

The sins especially emphasized are those of the priests and prophets who duped the people into a false security and in so doing were responsible for the shedding of blood (2:14; 4:13-16). This sin is more excoriated than the cannibalism into which many of the famine-reduced citizens fell — the latter being described rather as a shameful effect than a cause of the catastrophe (2:20; 4:10).

#4. Shame

The suffering of the prophet and the city is also articulated by the motif of shame. True in a general sense of all her deprivations, it is expressed especially by the gloating of enemies over her (1:7; 2:15-16; 3:14, 45-46) and her sense of nakedness (1:8).

#5. God as first cause

Related to the conviction that Judah's downfall is a punishment for sin is the unquestioned principle that God is the cause of all. Such a statement can stand beside that of total and free human responsibility, as it often does in the prophets (e.g., Jer 3:12; 24:7) without suggesting any inconsistency. Nor is Lamentations different from the rest of the Bible in its absence of neat distinction between God's direct and permissive will. Likewise, there are times when the secondary causes (in this case the Babylonian armies) are completely ignored and Yahweh is depicted as himself destroying the city and slaying her sons. The motif is too ubiquitous to detail here, but a quick glance at the second Lamentation, where Yahweh is subject of nearly half the sentences, will suffice to illustrate the point.

This radical approach no doubt accentuates the image of God as a wrathful avenger. The poet does not hesitate to accuse Yahweh of trampling out the blood of his people like the treader of a wine press (1:15). Yet this must be balanced by the statements that Yahweh's scourge is temporary, that though he punishes he will take pity, that he will not forget forever his covenant loyalty, and that "he has no joy in afflicting the sons of men" (3:31-33). The juxtaposition of these statements with the other principle five verses later to the effect that "from the mouth of the Most High proceed good and evil" (3:38) seems indeed to pose some kind of distinction like that formulated in a later era as God's primary will and permissive will. But in Lamentations the problem remains a problem in the bosom of the transcendent God. Job will later give it a more acute treatment, particularly concerning the suffering of the just, which is not the problem in Lamentations, for Jerusalem had sinned. But at the end Job's answer will be no better than that already intuited in Lamentations.

The positive fruit of this faith in Yahweh's omnipotence appears at the conclusion to the book. If God's hand has worked disaster, he can also achieve the necessary moral miracle which alone will make restoration possible: "Turn us to you and we shall be turned" (5:21).

It is the conviction that God is the master of the future that explains also the glimpse which Lamentations gives of the expiatory value of Judah's suffering and thereby sets the stage for the redemptive theology of the Servant Songs. Judah has expiated her sins (4:22); there is no direction now to go but up. And the trusting submission to the hand of God recommended by Lamentations (3:25-27, 30) prepares that trait emphasized by Second Isaiah in his description of the Suffering Servant (Is 50:6-9; 53:7-8).

#6. The Day of the Lord

Another significant contribution to the theology of the Old Testament is the poet's conception of promise and fulfillment, which appears in the "Day of the Lord" motif. The belief had apparently been widespread, even before the time of Amos, that the Day of the Lord was to be one of God's intervention in a miraculous way in favor of his people, but quite unrelated to any moral conversion on their part. Amos, we know, reacted against this supine complacency and stressed that the day was to be one of impartial judgment from which Israel herself would not escape (Amos 5:18-20). Isaiah and Zephaniah carried on this prophetic tradition (Is 2:12; Zeph 1:10-12). The exact phrase "Day of Yahweh" does not appear in Lamentations, but the prophetic teaching underlies its equivalent terms: "the day of his fierce anger" (1:12), "the day of his anger" (2:1), "the day of your anger" (2:21), "the day of Yahweh's anger" (2:22). Like the classical prophets, too, Lamentations considers the day of Yahweh as future (1:21). But what is absolutely unique about Lamentations in the Bible is that the Day of Yahweh is now regarded also as *past*. It has happened in the catastrophe which the poet describes. And yet it is obvious that the fall of Jerusalem was not the end of world history. Rather, what this double and seemingly contradictory affirmation implies is that "the day" is a mystery which admits of a partial fulfillment *now* which, in turn, anticipates a complete fulfillment in the *future*. The poet recognizes that in the actual working out of the prophetic promise of the "Day of Yahweh" there has been a split in the divine timetable, by which the day has already arrived for Judah, and is still to come for the nations. The significance of this insight for the interpretation of sacred history cannot be overestimated. It is exactly the same kind of fulfillment-promise that is affirmed by the New Testament (cf. O. Cullmann, *Christ and Time*, Philadelphia, 1950).

#7. Hope

In spite of the thorough desolation — or rather, because of it — the poet voices a strong hope for the future. Unlike Second Isaiah, the author of Lamentations has no human intermediary, like Cyrus, as the basis of his hope. It is Yahweh alone who is the foundation of hope (3:24), and the humbling of the soul before the goodness of Yahweh means that man may still look for redemption as a grace (3:29). The poet hopes for a universal judgment to come (1:21-22; 3:34-36, 64; 4:21-22), for an end to the exile (4:22), for political and religious restoration (5:21). The ground for this hope, as mentioned above, is that Judah's own sins, so grave as to raise the doubt whether forgiveness is possible (3:42; 5:22), have indeed been expiated in the suffering Judah has now undergone (4:22).

#8. Prayer

Hope is expressed chiefly in prayer. With the exception of chapter 4, each of the Lamentations concludes with a direct address to Yahweh. There are other insistent supplications which periodically interrupt the description of calamity, or merely ask Yahweh to *look* and consider (2:20). The entire book is an example and a lesson in the value of intercessory prayer for a specific object, with the importunity later to be recommended in the New Testament (Lk 18:1-8; 1 Th 5:17).

These motifs alone suffice to show the importance of the Book of Lamentations in the progress of revelation. We have already noted the influence the book would have on Second Isaiah. The latter is not only dependent on the Jerusalem poet for many elements of his theology, especially for the personalizing of national suffering and the confident, silent trust in Yahweh (Lam 3) which prepared the Servant Songs, but also for the structure and form of entire poems (cf. Is 47). Because of its critical position at the watershed between suffering and restoration (belonging more to the side of suffering, as Second Isaiah would to the side of restoration), it is little wonder that it should have an important liturgical function in the penitential liturgy of both Judaism and Christianity — the Jewish 9th of Ab commemorating the fall of the temple, and the Christian Good Friday commemorating the death of the Suffering Servant. But the hope to which it clings also explains why in Jewish liturgy from the 14th century onwards, Isaiah 40, the message of consolation by the anonymous prophet of the return, is read immediately after the Lamentations on the 9th of Ab.

THE BOOK OF LAMENTATIONS

Text and Commentary

FIRST LAMENTATION
Lam 1:1-22

1 How lonely she is now,
  the once crowded city!
Widowed is she
  who was mistress over nations;
The princess among the provinces
  has been made a toiling slave.

2 Bitterly she weeps at night,
  tears upon her cheeks,
With not one to console her
  of all her dear ones;
Her friends have all betrayed her
  and become her enemies.

This lament falls into two parts, 1-11 and 12-22. With minor exceptions, it is the poet who speaks in the first part, giving a vivid description of the city, and Sion who voices her grief in the second part. Following the traditional pattern, the dirge ends in a prayer (20-22).

1 The first verse consists of three contrasts between Jerusalem's present distress and her former glory, the order of presentation being reversed in the final line to heighten the effect and to leave the listener with the scene of the present disaster. "How" is the typical form for introducing a dirge; "she is" is literally, "she sits." Jerusalem had been described by the prophets as the spouse of Yahweh; now she is like a widow, not because Yahweh has died, but because his chastisement has left her with the sense of abandonment, all previous supports having been swept away — the temple, which she regarded as the visible sacrament of Yahweh's presence, and the throngs that circulated in the city on her feasts.

Lam
2:1; 4:1

Is 1:21

#1

2 Night is the time for love, but now instead of giving herself to her lovers (the states that supported her against Babylon), she can only weep. Her friends have been fickle.

#1 #2
Jer 27:3;
37;5-8

3 V. 3a seems to refer to those Judeans who preferred to

3Juda has fled into exile
    from oppression and cruel slavery;
Yet where she lives among the nations
    she finds no place to rest:
All her persecutors come upon her
    where she is narrowly confined.

4The roads to Sion mourn
    for lack of pilgrims going to her feasts;
All her gateways are deserted,
    her priests groan,
Her virgins sigh;
    she is in bitter grief.

5Her foes are uppermost,
    her enemies are at ease;
The Lord has punished her
    for her many sins.
Her little ones have gone away,
    captive before the foe.

6Gone from daughter Sion
    is all her glory:
Her princes, like rams
    that find no pasture,
Have gone off without strength
    before their captors.

go into exile rather than endure the bitter yoke of their over-   Jer 42-43
lords in Palestine; but their lot is no better.

4   The vitality of Jerusalem was once measured by the pilgrims pouring from the roads through the gates into the city.
These are now personified as weeping because of their deser-   Amos 6:1;
tion. "Zion" stands not merely for the mount but for the entire   Is 1:27
city. The city gate was the center of civic activity and of news.   Jer 14:2
In keeping with the liturgical dimension of this verse, virgins
are mentioned along with priests because they can no longer   Ps 68:26
play joyous roles in the processions.   Jer 31:13

5   For the first time the moral cause of her downfall is introduced: the Hebrew for *sins* here suggests a real activity of   #3
transgression, not a mere failure to live up to an expected
norm. The accusation is sandwiched gently between the
exalted position of the foe and the captivity of Israel's children.

6   Again personified as a woman, this time in the frequent   #1
term "daughter," Zion poignantly feels the loss of her glory
and her leaders.

7   To the modern reader, it seems as though v. 7 looks back   #4
on the suffering from a distance. All the verbs in the verse are

7Jerusalem is mindful of the days
  of her wretched homelessness,
When her people fell into enemy hands,
  and she had no one to help her;
When her foes gloated over her,
  laughed at her ruin.

8Through the sin of which she is guilty,
  Jerusalem is defiled;
All who esteemed her think her vile
  now that they see her nakedness;
She herself groans
  and turns away.

9Her filth is on her skirt;
  she gave no thought how she would end.
Astounding is her downfall,
  with no one to console her.
Look, O Lord, upon her misery,
  for the enemy has triumphed!

10The foe stretched out his hand
  to all her treasures;
She has seen those nations
  enter her sanctuary
Whom you forbade to come
  into your assembly.

11All her people groan,
  searching for bread;
They give their treasures for food,
  to retain the breath of life.
"Look, O Lord, and see
  how worthless I have become!

in the same tense, however, and have to do with present
misery.

8   Again the source of Zion's misery is found in her sin —   #3 #4
with the emphatic "sinned a sin" in the Hebrew. The exposure
of nakedness is a common prophetic motif for the shame pre-
cipitated by sin; she turns her back so as to be less exposed   Jer 13:22,
to the gaze of her former lovers.   26

9   The sin of the city, still personified as a woman, is likened
to filth on the skirt. The poet climaxes the emotion by having the city speak, "Look, O Lord, upon my misery. . . ."   #8

10   Nebuchadnezzar's armies looted the temple treasures — de-   2 Chr
scribed here in slow motion as "stretching forth his hand" —   36:10,
the apex of his violation which began when he crossed the   19
temple precincts forbidden to Gentiles.   Ez 44:9
                                                                   Jer 51:51
11   Racked by the pangs of famine, the inhabitants give their

12"Come, all you who pass by the way,
    look and see
Whether there is any suffering like my suffering,
    which has been dealt me
When the Lord afflicted me
    on the day of his blazing wrath.

13"From on high he sent fire
    down into my very frame;
He spread a net for my feet,
    and overthrew me.
He left me desolate,
    in pain all the day.

14"He has kept watch over my sins;
    by his hand they have been plaited:
They have settled about my neck,
    he has brought my strength to its knees;
The Lord has delivered me into their grip,
    I am unable to rise.

15"All the mighty ones in my midst
    the Lord has cast away;
He summoned an army against me
    to crush my young men;
The Lord has trodden in the wine press
    virgin daughter Juda.

16"At this I weep,
    my eyes run with tears:
Far from me are all who could console me,
    any who might revive me;
My sons were reduced to silence
    when the enemy prevailed."

jewels in exchange for food. The last line articulates the city's groaning. #8 #5

12   The afflicted widow now turns to the passers-by for compassion. This line is used frequently in the Christian liturgy of Holy Week. The "Day of Yahweh" appears here as already having arrived for Jerusalem, in the sense which the prophets, beginning with Amos, had predicted. Amos 5:18ff Zeph 1:10-12 #5

13   Unabashedly the poet piles up figures of chastisement, attributing them all directly to Yahweh. From on high, Yahweh rained fire (frequent image for God's wrath) and trampled it into her very bones. The spreading of a net is a frequent figure in the Old Testament. Ez 12:13 Hos 7:12

14   The image here used is that of bringing an animal under subjection and service by preparing and fastening the thongs of the yoke. Used primarily for draft animals, a yoke was oc-

17Sion stretched out her hands,
   but there was no one to console her;
The Lord gave orders against Jacob
   for his neighbors to be his foes;
Jerusalem has become in their midst
   a thing unclean.

18"The Lord is just;
   I had defied his command.
Listen, all you peoples,
   and behold my suffering:
My maidens and my youths
   have gone into captivity.

19"I cried out to my lovers,
   but they failed me.
My priests and my elders
   perished in the city;
Where they sought food for themselves,
   they found it not.

20"Look, O Lord, upon my distress:
   all within me is in ferment,
My heart recoils within me
   from my monstrous rebellion.
In the streets the sword bereaves,
   at home death stalks.

21"Give heed to my groaning;
   there is no one to console me.

casionally used on captives and slaves, and hence became a a figure for servitude, particularly of one nation to another. Here again, the yoke is basically that of Judah's sins. [Gn 27:40; Jer 27:8 #3]

15-16   The Hebrew *mo'ed*, here translated *army*, ordinarily means a religious assembly; the thought may be, as in Zephaniah, that Yahweh has called a sacrificial feast, with Judah herself the victim. The Hebrew for "crush" is striking here, for nowhere else in the Bible is it used with animate beings as its object. The image is made more gruesome by depicting Yahweh as crushing the virgin city so that her blood runs out like juice from grapes trodden in the winepress. [Zeph 1:7-8 #5 #2]

17   The direct discourse is interrupted as the poet describes the collapsed kingdom, alternately called Zion, Jacob, and Jerusalem. Jacob is, strictly speaking, a title for the Northern Kingdom, but like Israel is sometimes used for Judah also. Yahweh is the commander-in-chief of the enemy armies against his own city. Edom, among others, cooperated in the looting and ravaging of Jerusalem. [#5]

All my enemies rejoice at my misfortune:
  it is you who have wrought it.
Bring on the day you have proclaimed,
  that they may be even as I.

22"Let all their evil come before you;
    deal with them
As you have dealt with me
    for all my sins;
My groans are many,
    and I am sick at heart."

2 How the Lord in his wrath
    has detested daughter Sion!
He has cast down from heaven to earth
    the glory of Israel,
Unmindful of his footstool
    on the day of his wrath.

2The Lord has consumed without pity
    all the dwellings of Jacob;
He has torn down in his anger
    the fortresses of daughter Juda;
He has brought to the ground in dishonor
    her king and her princes.

3He broke off, in fiery wrath,
    the horn that was Israel's whole strength;
He withheld the support of his right hand
    when the enemy approached;

18-19   In the midst of this extreme agony, a brilliant cry of faith   #3 #2
emerges: God is just because Judah has violated the covenant,
thus bringing on herself the curse of captivity. The foreign   Dt. 28:41
allies, as the prophets had warned, failed to help her.   Jer 30:14

20   Jerusalem speaks as if the siege and the breakthrough were   #8
taking place at the moment. "Heart" is literally "bowels," the
seat of the emotions. Again it is her own rebellion not against   #3
Babylon but against Yahweh which is the source of her mis-   Dt 32:25
eries. There is no escape or refuge from calamity.

21-22   Here Yahweh's complete control of the situation is pressed.   #8
Though the Massoretic text reads, "You have brought on the   #5
Day," most scholars prefer the Syriac reading, "Bring on the
day," particularly in virtue of the terminal "that they may be
even as I," and the sense of the following verse. Hence, the
Day of Yahweh is seen both as past (v. 12) and as future —   #6
an important contribution to our understanding of the "fulfilled and unfulfilled" dimensions of the divine timetable. The
poet asks that the divine anger, which Judah has justly ex-

He blazed up in Jacob like a flaming fire
   devouring all about it.

4Like an enemy he made taut his bow;
   with his arrows in his right hand
He took his stand as a foe, and slew
   all on whom the eye doted;
Over the tent of daughter Sion
   he poured out his wrath like fire.

5The Lord has become an enemy,
   he has consumed Israel:
Consumed all her castles
   and destroyed her fortresses;
For daughter Juda he has multiplied
   moaning and groaning.

6He has demolished his shelter like a garden booth,
   he has destroyed his dwelling;
In Sion the Lord has made
   feast and Sabbath to be forgotten;
He has scorned in fierce wrath
   both king and priest.

perienced for her own sins, come upon her enemies for their   #3
sins.

SECOND LAMENTATION
Lam 2:1-22

The second Lamentation is less formal than the first and
the description more vivid. The theme of tragic reversal is   #1
more common; in that Yahweh is subject of nearly half the
sentences, his direct responsibility for Zion's plight is under-   #5
lined. The poet himself speaks throughout, even in the prayer
with which the Lamentation typically concludes.   # 1, 2, 5

1-2   The lament again begins with the usual "How. . . !" The   Is 13:19
"glory of Israel" is either the city or, more probably, the tem-   #1
ple. It was thought to have a heavenly abode, since Yahweh,   Is 64:10
who dwells in heaven, also dwelt in the temple. If heaven sup-   Ps 104:3
ported the throne of Yahweh, the temple, his footstool, was   Dt 12:5
kicked aside on that day. The king is Zedekiah.   1 Chr 28:2
                                                                     #6

3   The horn is a frequent biblical figure for power; not only   #5
did Yahweh fail to come to the aid of Zion, but he actually
flared up within it and devoured the neighborhood.

4   Yahweh has been like an enemy to Jerusalem. The no-   Jer 30:14
tables and the youth, lit., "all the desirable ones of the eye,"
he has slain. The "tent" of daughter Zion is the temple.   #2

7The Lord has disowned his altar,
  rejected his sanctuary;
The walls of her towers
  he has handed over to the enemy,
Who shout in the house of the Lord
  as on a feast day.

8The Lord marked for destruction
  the wall of daughter Sion:
He stretched out the measuring line;
  his hand brought ruin, yet he did not relent —
He brought grief on wall and rampart
  till both succumbed.

9Sunk into the ground are her gates;
  he has removed and broken her bars.
Her king and her princes are among the pagans;
  priestly instruction is wanting,
And her prophets have not received
  any vision from the Lord.

10On the ground in silence sit
  the old men of daughter Sion;

Yahweh is directly accused of being an enemy and himself #5 #2
consuming Israel.

6-7   The most incomprehensible event for Israel's faith was the
fall of the house of Yahweh. The reaction of faith was that
it had been destroyed by none but Yahweh himself, with the #5
ease and perfection with which a harvester knocks down the
temporary shelter he has set up in a field. More incompre- Is 1:8
hensible still, Yahweh has made it impossible to celebrate his
Sabbath and his own feasts with their usual solemnity: both Ez 24:21
political and religious institutions have been swept away.

8   Stretching the measuring line or the plummet was a gesture #2 #5
used not only in preparing to build but also in marking off 2 K 21:13;
what was to be destroyed.   Amos 7:7-9
                                                               Is 34:11
9   The gates' bars, broken and missing, were partially buried
under the rubble of collapsed walls. True to the Deuteronomic threat, king and leaders have gone into exile. It was Dt 28:36
the priests' duty to give instruction, as it was the prophets'
to relate visions of the Lord. Through these means Yahweh   Jer 18:18
came to his people, made known to them his will and what
was to be done next. But now he comes to them through   Ez 7:26
no medium at all. The complaint that there is no prophet with
a message could hardly have come from Jeremiah, who continued to prophesy.

> They strew dust on their heads
> and gird themselves with sackcloth;
> The maidens of Jerusalem
> bow their heads to the ground.

11 Worn out from weeping are my eyes,
within me all is in ferment;
My gall is poured out on the ground
because of the downfall of the daughter of my people,
As child and infant faint away
in the open spaces of the town.

12 They ask their mothers,
"Where is the cereal?" — in vain,
As they faint away like the wounded
in the streets of the city,
And breathe their last
in their mothers' arms.

13 To what can I liken or compare you,
O daughter Jerusalem?
What example can I show you for your comfort,
virgin daughter Sion?
For great as the sea is your downfall;
who can heal you?

14 Your prophets had for you
false and specious visions;
They did not lay bare your guilt,
to avert your fate;
They beheld for you in vision
false and misleading portents.

10   As the people looked to the priests for instruction and
to the prophets for oracles, they looked to the elders of the   Ez 7:26
city for counsel. These now sit in silence and in a gesture   Jb 2:12
of penance. The maidens of "daughter of Zion" throw them-   #2
selves to the ground in despair.

11-12   As he begins the second part of the lament, the poet gives   Lam 3:48
vent to his personal feelings. The pouring out of one's gall is
biblical image for extreme sorrow. To what extent the ex-   Jb 16:13
pression "daughter" had come to stand for the city can be
seen in the variation of "Daughter Zion" to "daughter of my   #2
people." Homeless children wander about the streets and
collapse in the city squares. They keep asking the same ques-   Lam 1:11
tion (the Hebrew imperfect of frequentative action).

13   From this verse onward, the poet addresses the city itself,   Lam 1:12
again with the tender term "daughter." The verse ends with   #2
a question thrown into the depths of her sorrow: who can
heal you? No answer is immediately given; it would be hard

15All who pass by
    clap their hands at you;
They hiss and wag their heads
    over daughter Jerusalem:
"Is this the all-beautiful city,
    the joy of the whole earth?"

16All your enemies
    open their mouths against you;
They hiss and gnash their teeth.
    They say, "We have devoured her.
This at last is the day we hoped for;
    we have lived to see it!"

17The Lord has done as he decreed:
    he has fulfilled the threat
He set forth from days of old;
    he has destroyed and had no pity,
Letting the enemy gloat over you
    and exalting the horn of your foes.

18Cry out to the Lord;
    moan, O daughter Sion!
Let your tears flow like a torrent
    day and night;
Let there be no respite for you,
    no repose for your eyes.

19Rise up, shrill in the night,
    at the beginning of every watch;
Pour out your heart like water
    in the presence of the Lord;

to console a person whose grief is as chaotic and deep as the sea. But the traditional sources of light and consolation are excluded as bankrupt, proven so, as Jeremiah had promised, by the outcome of the events. Most significant of their failures was their unwillingness to put their finger on the real center of her trouble, her guilt. *Jer 23:9ff* *#3*

15-16 Again the taunts of the passers-by and the victors are recorded, contrasting fallen Jerusalem with her former glory and gloating over the conquest. *#1, 2, 4* *Lam 3:46*

17 The Deuteronomic curse upon those who violate the covenant has been proved a reality. *#5, 3* *Dt 28:15*

18-19 All Zion can do is to pray intensely and incessantly, and this is what the poet urges. The night, calculated from six in the evening till six in the morning, was divided into three watches of four hours each. The prayer is not only that of repentance but also of intercession with a glimmer of hope. *#8, 2* *Jg 7:19* *#7*

20-22 The city answers the poet's invitation and prays to Yah-

Lift up your hands to him
for the lives of your little ones
[Who faint from hunger
at the corner of every street].

20"Look, O Lord, and consider:
whom have you ever treated thus?
Must women eat their offspring,
their well-formed children?
Are priest and prophet to be slain
in the sanctuary of the Lord?

21"Dead in the dust of the streets
lie young and old;
My maidens and young men
have fallen by the sword;
You have slain on the day of your wrath,
slaughtered without pity.

22"You summoned as for a feast day
terrors against me from all sides;
There was not, on the day of your wrath,
either fugitive or survivor;
Those whom I bore and reared
my enemy has utterly destroyed."

weh, thus concluding the second lament as the first: "Look!"
the city cries, knowing that for God to look is to answer.
Two of the most dreadful scourges are laid before Yahweh's
gaze: the cannibalism to which the fierce hunger drove many   Bar 2:3
of the inhabitants and the slaying of priests and prophets in   Ez 5:10
his very sanctuary. The whole historical tragedy is read in the
light of the prophets: it is God who has acted to punish the   #5
people's sins. This lament does not end with a prayer for vengeance, as do the first and third laments; it carries only a
final striking complaint. Yahweh has summoned to Jerusalem
as many terrors as formerly there had been pilgrims for the
feasts. The day of his wrath has descended upon the city,   #6
and those whom she, like a mother, spent such efforts at bear-   #2
ing and rearing, are now liquidated.

THIRD LAMENTATION

Lam 3:1-64

The third lament is likewise an alphabetical poem, but with
three verses instead of merely one beginning with the same
Hebrew letter. This explains why in our numbering system
there are 66 verses, whereas in the previous hymns there
were only 22. But this is not the only difference. At first sight,

3 I am a man who knows affliction
    from the rod of his anger,
2One whom he has led and forced to walk
    in darkness, not in the light;
3Against me alone he brings back his hand
    again and again all the day.

4He has worn away my flesh and my skin,
    he has broken my bones;
5He has beset me round about
    with poverty and weariness;
6He has left me to dwell in the dark
    like those long dead.

7He has hemmed me in with no escape
    and weighed me down with chains;
8Even when I cry out for help,
    he stops my prayer;
9He has blocked my ways with fitted stones,
    and turned my paths aside.

10A lurking bear he has been to me,
    a lion in ambush!
11He deranged my ways, set me astray,
    left me desolate.

it seems that this third chapter is the voice of an individual poet or prophet expressing his own personal anguish. Vv. 48-51 lend support to this interpretation, for there the "I" appears in contrast with the city and the people. On the other hand, there is repeated reference to national suffering, particularly beginning with v. 40, where the "we" and "us" return. The critics have thus been divided between a collective interpretation (R. Smend, E. Kautzsch, G. Beer) and an individual interpretation (B. Stade, K. Budde, M. Lohr, T. Meek). In the midst of the discussion, several possible ways of breaking down the parts of the chapter have been suggested, on the assumption that the author used pre-existing psalms and tailored them to his purpose. The major difficulty with such an interpretation is that the author would have had a tortuous job of working such materials into the perfect alphabetical psalm he offers us.

It seems, therefore, preferable to find the explanation of the uniqueness and the diversity of form in the intention of the poet. He wishes to stir up repentance and submission and to kindle the embers of hope buried under the ashes of disaster. Poet himself, he had no need to incorporate previous psalms, but he was well acquainted with the styles of the in-

12He bent his bow, and set me up
  as the target for his arrow.
13He pierces my sides
  with shafts from his quiver.
14I have become a laughingstock for all nations,
  their taunt all the day long;
15He has sated me with bitter food,
  made me drink my fill of wormwood.

dividual lament, the song of trust, and the national lament.
He concentrates the images of suffering in personal terms to
make them as poignant as possible (1-20), then springs into
a song of trust (21-33), an exhortation to see the hand of
God in it all (34-39), a national lament (40-47), returning
to what is chiefly an individual lament (48-66). But none of
these forms is pure. Far from attributing the fluctuation from
individual to collective to the ineptitude of the poet, it makes
much better sense to understand them in the light of the
Hebrew concept of corporate personality and the uniqueness
of the situation in which the poet wrote, which led him to
marshall several poetic forms and to mix them as the emotion
seemed to suggest. Thus, for example, the poet sees no inconsistency in saying, "It is good for a *man* to bear the yoke
from his youth" (v. 27) and "Let us search and examine *our*
ways that we may return to the Lord!" (40). Nor does he
find any inconsistency in varying the images for the people
between feminine (daughter) and masculine (man, v. 1),
just as in the second song (where Jacob-Israel occurs for
the masculine).

In the third poem more than in any other, the author re-
duces the whole of his suffering to the hand of Yahweh, #5
(cf. Introduction). Likewise it is here that there emerges the
most confident hope for renewal. The importance of this #7
poem is underlined not only by its unusual alphabetic form
but also by the central position it occupies in the five Lamentations.

1-3 The poet speaks both in his own name and for his people, seeing one mystery of suffering. It is only moderns who
find difficult the transition from the feminine images of widow
and daughter in the first two laments to "I am a man." Hosea,
famous for his description of Israel as the wife, also called   Hos 11:1
the people God's "son" whom he called from Egypt. The
later Servant-Songs of Isaiah will variously describe Judah   Is 52:1f;
as a daughter, a woman, a herald, and a servant. Neverthe-   54:1ff; 51:
                                                               17ff; 41:8ff

> 16He has broken my teeth with gravel,
>   pressed my face in the dust;
> 17My soul is deprived of peace,
>   I have forgotten what happiness is;
> 18I tell myself my future is lost,
>   all that I hoped for from the Lord.
>
> 19The thought of my homeless poverty
>   is wormwood and gall;

less, those critics are correct who maintain that the cries here are not merely the poetic personification of the national grief, but the real personal sufferings of the speaker in whom the collectivity is embodied.

In the opening lines, God is not expressly named but is the anonymous "he." The light-darkness theme, frequent in the psalms, is rarer in Lamentations. The *hand* here is not the expression of victorious might but of the heavy weight of affliction.

4-6 Flesh and bones express a totality but to some extent no doubt reflect the emaciated state to which most of the inhabitants, including probably the poet himself, were reduced. At this stage of revelation, the dead were thought to abide in a region of darkness. This line is a direct quotation of the psalm, with the order of the first two words reversed to fit the acrostic. *(Jb 30:30; Is 38:13; Ps 143:3)*

7-9 Yahweh has walled the man in as a prisoner and fettered him, lit., "made my bronze heavy." Not only are there no physical ways of escape but even the most spiritual prayer seems to have no issue. *(Jb 19:8; Ps 22:2)*

10-13 In perfect confirmation of Hosea's threat, God has attacked like a bear or a lion in ambush. The audacity of the comparison would be blasphemous were not the poet conscious also that such treatment was deserved. The figure of the archer presses the ill-treatment: the "sides" are literally "the kidneys," organs that are sensitive and also, in Hebrew thought, the seat of life. *(Hos 13:8; Jb 10:16)*

14-16 Humiliation and bitterness return in these verses. Wormwood is a plant whose leaves have a very bitter taste. Jeremiah had predicted Jerusalem's suffering in precisely these terms. To them the poet adds that his food had been gravel on which he has broken his teeth. *(#4; Jer 9:14; 23:15)*

17-18 The thought advances significantly as the poet voices his discouragement, his feeling that the future, including all the good things and the prosperity he hoped for from the Lord, *(#7)*

20Remembering it over and over
  leaves my soul downcast within me.
21But I will call this to mind,
  as my reason to have hope:

22The favors of the Lord are not exhausted,
  his mercies are not spent;
23They are renewed each morning,
  so great is his faithfulness.
24My portion is the Lord, says my soul;
  therefore will I hope in him.

25Good is the Lord to one who waits for him,
  to the soul that seeks him;
26It is good to hope in silence
  for the saving help of the Lord.
27It is good for a man to bear
  the yoke from his youth.

28Let him sit alone and in silence,
  when it is laid upon him.
29Let him put his mouth to the dust;
  there may yet be hope.
30Let him offer his cheek to be struck,
  let him be filled with disgrace.

is lost. Here, for the first time in the lament, does he mention the divine name, Yahweh.

19-21   The same thought is repeated, but, almost as if suddenly illumined by the thought of the divine Name, the poet in the nadir of despair finds the foundation of divine hope, which he will now detail.   #7

22-24   A truly remarkable confession, the statement is of broadest application; in the immediate context, however, it would seem to mean that it is a grace that his people have not been totally annihilated, since such is what they deserved.   Neh 9:31

Above all his bitterness the poet's faith in God's *ḥesed* stands pure and strong. The Hebrew *ḥeleq*, "portion," can mean the *lot* which is apportioned to one in life, or inheritance. In either case, what the poet is affirming here is that, though he is deprived of home and wealth and prosperity, there is one reality to which he clings now more firmly than ever: the Lord. The short phrase, "My portion is the Lord," emerging in the midst of the chaos which has all but buried the poet and his nation, is like the discovery of a shining coin suddenly rubbed clean of mud. It is most significant that there is absolutely no human fulcrum on which this hope could rest, neither present nor in the foreseeable future. No   Pss 16:5; 73:26

31For the Lord's rejection
  does not last forever;
32Though he punishes, he takes pity,
  in the abundance of his mercies;
33He has no joy in afflicting
  or grieving the sons of men.

34When anyone tramples underfoot
  all the prisoners in the land,
35When he distorts men's rights
  in the very sight of the Most High,
36When he presses a crooked claim,
  the Lord does not look on unconcerned.

37Who commands, so that it comes to pass,
  except the Lord ordains it;
38Except it proceeds from the mouth of the Most High,
  whether the thing be good or bad!
39Why should any living man complain,
  any mortal, in the face of his sins?

40Let us search and examine our ways
  that we may return to the Lord!
41Let us reach out our hearts
  toward God in heaven!

mystic of the Dark Night of the soul has since expressed   **#7**
more succinctly the essence of pure faith and hope.

25-27   The thrice repeated *tob* lines up three things that are *good*:
first, Yahweh himself, who is good to those who earnestly
wait for and seek him; second, hoping in silence
for God's saving help; third, bearing the yoke from one's   **Jer 2:20**
youth — the latter expression meaning to do God's will and
to accept the trials that he sends.

28-30   These verses are the first intuition of what will be developed in the Servant-Songs of Second Isaiah; it is not a
masochistic relishing of suffering but a realization that in
God's plan it must have meaning and a redemptive outcome:
"there may still be hope." (The conditional phrasing in-   **#4, 7**
dicates man has no *right* to God's mercy but awaits it as a   **Is 50:6;**
grace.) And this leads to a willing acceptance of and submis-   **Mt 5:39**
sion to present suffering.

31-33   The first motive for this submission is that the suffering
is only temporary; this insight in turn is based on the theo-   **Ps 103:9;**
logical principle that Yahweh can take no pleasure in punish-   **Rom 11:1**
ment for its own sake. If he does punish, it is, as it were, like
a father who takes no delight in punishing a disobedient child
and does so only for the child's own good and correction.

42We have sinned and rebelled;
  you have not forgiven us.

43You veiled yourself in wrath and pursued us,
  you slew us and took no pity;
44You wrapped yourself in a cloud
  which prayer could not pierce.
45You have made us offscourings and refuse
  among the nations.

46All our enemies
  have opened their mouths against us;
47Terror and the pit have been our lot,
  desolation and destruction;
48My eyes run with streams of water
  over the downfall of the daughter of my people.

49My eyes flow without ceasing,
  there is no respite,
50Till the Lord from heaven
  looks down and sees.
51My eyes torment my soul
  at the sight of all the daughters of my city.

52Those who were my enemies without cause
  hunted me down like a bird;
53They struck me down alive in the pit,
  and sealed me in with a stone.
54The waters flowed over my head,
  and I said, "I am lost!"

Hosea had already depicted the heart of Yahweh torn be- Hos 11
tween the need for correcting and the desire to show mercy.

34-36 The second motive for abandonment to God is that nothing happens without his knowledge. This means two things:
(a) *for the oppressors*: God measures their crime and marks
them for eventual punishment. "In the very sight of the Most
High" perhaps refers to doing this in the city of God's temple.

37-39 (b) *for Judah*: since nothing happens without God's permission, and it has already been established that his purpose is correction, Judah should think more of her sins
which have brought upon her this tragedy. When men
(*'adam*) think of the enormity of their sins, what motive
have they to complain? The thought here is universal and
not merely confined to the covenant people. Likewise the
exalted role of God creator, by whose mere word things are Is 45:7
or cease to be, thrusts toward the creation theology of Sec- 40:26;
ond Isaiah and Genesis 1. 43:1

40-41 Now making his identification with the people explicit by
using the first person plural, the poet exhorts his brothers to

55I called upon your name, O Lord,
    from the bottom of the pit;
56You heard me call, "Let not your ear
    be deaf to my cry for help!"
57You came to my aid when I called to you;
    you said, "Have no fear!"

58You defended me in mortal danger,
    you redeemed my life.
59You see, O Lord, how I am wronged;
    do me justice!
60You see all their vindictiveness,
    all their plots against me.

61You hear their insults, O Lord,
    [all their plots against me],
62The whispered murmurings of my foes,
    against me all the day;
63Whether they sit or stand,
    see, I am their taunt song.

64Requite them as they deserve, O Lord,
    according to their deeds;
65Give them hardness of heart,
    as your curse upon them;
66Pursue them in wrath and destroy them
    from under your heavens!

examine their conduct as the first step in returning to Yahweh. The trial has impressed them once again with the transcendence of God who now is accessible only in heaven (his earthly abode has been destroyed).

42-44 But so far there has been no forgiveness; God has wrapped himself in a cloud of wrath which prayer has been unable

45-51 to penetrate. Proof of this situation is found again in the present humiliation which Judah is suffering. But the poet persists in prayer, thrice proclaiming his weeping, trusting that eventually he will be heard. Most poignant is the sight of the women and the maidens of the city who are defenseless before the conquerors.   Lam 2:16 #4 #7 #2 #8

52-54 The poet now describes his past sufferings in terms reminiscent of Jeremiah in prison and in the miry cistern.   Jer 37:16; 38:6-9

55-63 In that situation Jeremiah called upon the Lord and his prayer was answered both by the consoling voice which banished fear and by active intervention which saved his life. Now our poet makes a similar petition, appealing to God's sense of justice. Since he has already admitted sin,   Ps 130:1f #8 Ps 35:23f

4 How tarnished is the gold,
 how changed the noble metal;
How the sacred stones lie strewn
 at every street corner!

2 Sion's precious sons,
 fine gold their counterpart,
Now worth no more than earthen jars
 made by the hands of a potter!

3 Even the jackals bare their breasts
 and suckle their young;
The daughter of my people has become as cruel
 as the ostrich in the desert.

4 The tongue of the suckling cleaves
 to the roof of its mouth in thirst;
The babes cry for food,
 but there is no one to give it to them.

it can hardly be that his suffering is unjust; but neither is the oppression by the enemy just in God's eyes. The "you see . . . you see . . . you hear . . ." repeats the poet's faith in God's perfect knowledge of the situation and urges him to act in view of this knowledge. "Sitting" and "standing" means both in idleness and at work—therefore all the time.

64-66   The Lamentation ends with a vindictive prayer, which to a   Ps 28:4 modern mind formed by later revelation seems anti-climactic, especially after the heights to which the poem has risen. The horizon of this poem then is that suffering is to be accepted from God and submitted to humbly; but a just vengeance upon the oppressor who was the instrument of that suffering was still something that could be prayed for. Jeremiah, the great suffering poet-prophet, was not able to rise   Jer 11:20 higher. The message to love the enemy, to do good to those who show hatred, and to pray *for* the persecutors instead of   Mt 5:44 against them was as yet unheard, as was the voice from the Cross, "Father, forgive them, for they know not what they   Lk 23:34 are doing."

FOURTH LAMENTATION
Lam 4:1-22

The fourth song resembles the second in many ways; more than any, however, it stresses the theme of tragic reversal,   #1 to which the entire first eight verses are devoted. The imagery

⁵Those accustomed to dainty food
   perish in the streets;
Those brought up in purple
   now cling to the ash heaps.

⁶The punishment of the daughter of my people
   is greater than the penalty of Sodom,
Which was overthrown in an instant
   without the turning of a hand.

⁷Brighter than snow were her princes,
   whiter than milk,
More ruddy than coral,
   more precious than sapphire.

⁸Now their appearance is blacker than soot,
   they are unrecognized on the streets;
Their skin shrinks on their bones,
   as dry as wood.

is vivid and concrete, that of an eye-witness. The lament is especially severe on the priests and prophets who are responsible for misleading and even exploiting the people with rank injustice.

1-2 Again the introductory "How!" presents the contrast of Jerusalem's former glory with her present state. The gold and stones of holiness, indicative of the temple treasures, are in reality the inhabitants of Jerusalem, described in the second verse — a distant preparation for 1 Peter's use of "living stones" for the people of God.

1:1; 2:1
#1

1 Pt 2:5

3-4 The poet now zeroes in on the greatest moral weakness which famine and distress revealed in the citizens of the city: abandonment of children. Even the jackal, mangy and drawn in the desert drought, will suckle its young; but the "daughter of my people" has become like the ostrich, which, according to popular belief, abandoned her eggs once she had laid them in the sand.

#2
Jb 39:14ff

5 The nobles brought up on dainty food and the royalty once clothed in purple now haunt the city dumps. Such tragic reversal, like the temptation to cannibalism, was part of the Deuteronomic curse for violation of the covenant.

#1

Dt 28:56f

6 Sodom's destruction was instantaneous; that of Jerusalem long and agonizing. Sodom perished directly by God's hand; Jerusalem by the instrument of a barbaric foe.

Gn 19:23f

7-8 The leaders, whose robust health shone with the brightness of snow and the whiteness of milk, glittering like coral and sapphire, now are charred with death and ashen with famine.

#1
Lam 3:4

9Better for those who perish by the sword
　　than for those who die of hunger,
Who waste away, as though pierced through,
　　lacking the fruits of the field!

10The hands of compassionate women
　　boiled their own children,
To serve them as mourners' food
　　in the downfall of the daughter of my people.

11The Lord has spent his anger,
　　poured out his blazing wrath;
He has kindled a fire in Sion
　　that has consumed her foundations.

12The kings of the earth did not believe,
　　nor any of the world's inhabitants,
That enemy or foe could enter
　　the gates of Jerusalem.

13Because of the sins of her prophets
　　and the crimes of her priests,
Who shed in her midst
　　the blood of the just! —

14They staggered blindly in the streets,
　　soiled with blood,
So that people could not touch
　　even their garments:

9-10　　A less painful death is that of the sword than that by
famine. Again the poet reiterates the horrors of cannibalism
to which women known for their compassion have now
turned.

#1
Lam 2:20;
Dt 28:56
2 K 6:29

11　　The destruction of Jerusalem is the work of God's anger
under its usual image of fire, which here may have the more
concrete reference to the burning of the city.

#5
2 Chr 36:19

12　　The nations are represented poetically as sharing in Judah's certitude that Jerusalem would never be destroyed. Jeremiah had inveighed against this disaster-begging complacency.

Jer 27:14

13　　As in the second Lamentation, the priests and the prophets are singled out as chiefly responsible for the city's downfall; here they are, moreover, accused of murder. There were
those indeed who plotted against the just, but the poet more
probably means to accuse them in a general way of precipi-
tating the mass slaughter of innocent inhabitants by their devi-
ous counsel.

Lam 2:14
#3

Jer 6:13

14-15　　Their moral filth is here compared with that of lepers,
who must go about crying "Unclean!" To be consistent with

15"Away, you unclean!" they cried to them,
   "Away, away, do not draw near!"
If they left and wandered among the nations,
   nowhere could they remain.

16The Lord himself has dispersed them,
   he regards them no more;
He does not receive the priests with favor,
   nor show kindness to the elders.

17Our eyes ever wasted away,
   looking in vain for aid;
From our watchtower we watched
   for a nation that could not save us.

18Men dogged our steps
   so that we could not walk in our streets;
Our end drew near, and came;
   our time had expired.

19Our pursuers were swifter
   than eagles in the air,
They harassed us on the mountains
   and waylaid us in the desert.

20The anointed one of the Lord, our breath of life,
   was caught in their snares,
He in whose shadow we thought
   we could live on among the nations.

the figure, it is the priests, not the people, who utter this cry. Unclean to their own people, they become fugitive like Cain and wander among the nations, where no one will let them settle. The effects of sin as separation from the community are thus graphically underlined. **Gn 4:14** **#3**

16   And neither to Yahweh are the priests and elders acceptable. The conclusion follows inevitably, it seems, from the fact that their dispersion happened, and it was the Lord's own doing. **#5**

17   Until the very last moments of the siege, Jerusalem awaited help from the Egyptians. **Jer 37:5ff**

18   From their siege-towers the Chaldeans eyed the streets and attacked the inhabitants who finally realized that the end had come.

19-20   At the last moment, King Zedekiah and some warriors escaped from the city in the direction of the desert but were arrested at Jericho. With the capture of the king expired the hopes that had been fixed on him. The king is here given two titles, one strictly Jewish, the "anointed of the Lord" (me-šiaḥ), the other borrowed from Egyptian usage, "our breath **2 K 25:4ff** **Jer 39:4ff**

21Though you rejoice and are glad, O daughter Edom,
  you who dwell in the land of Us,
To you also shall the cup be passed;
  you shall become drunk and naked.

22Your chastisement is completed, O daughter Sion,
  he will not prolong your exile;
But your wickedness, O daughter Edom, he will punish,
  he will lay bare your sins.

5 Remember, O Lord, what has befallen us,
    look, and see our disgrace:
2Our inherited lands have been turned over to strangers,
  our homes to foreigners.
3We have become orphans, fatherless;
  widowed are our mothers.

of life." Both focus on the hope of salvation or at least on survival among the nations which still seemed to be politically possible after the disaster of 598 B.C. But a decade later even her neighbors (v. 21) allied with Babylon to destroy her completely.

21-22   Instead of ending with a prayer as heretofore, the lament ends in a promise of doom for Edom, the most hated of Judah's neighbors. The bitterness was made more poignant by Edom's cooperation in Judah's downfall. Though Edom gloats now, her own hour is coming. The land of Uz is connected with Edom in several Old Testament texts; it was the home of Job. Meantime, the last line expresses the poet's relief that daughter Zion's own punishment for her sins has been completed. The poet foresees a short exile. It was this that enabled Second Isaiah to say, forty years later at the end of what he viewed as a long exile, "She has received from the hand of the Lord *double* for all her sins." But Edom's sins must still be laid bare by God's wrath and expiated.

Gn 36:28
1 Chr 1:42

#2

Is 40:2
#3

FIFTH LAMENTATION
Lam 5:1-22

This Lamentation is not really a dirge as the first, second, and third were, but rather a national prayer for God's mercy in the sense both of forgiveness and of restoration. The Vulgate properly understood its character by entitling it, "Prayer of the Prophet Jeremiah." Though it lacks the acrostic scheme, it is accommodated to the alphabetical style of the previous poems by having 22 verses, corresponding to the

#8

4The water we drink we must buy,
   for our own wood we must pay.
5On our necks is the yoke of those who drive us;
   we are worn out, but allowed no rest.

6To Egypt we submitted,
   and to Assyria, to fill our need of bread.
7Our fathers, who sinned, are no more;
   but we bear their guilt.
8Slaves rule over us;
   there is no one to rescue us from their hands.
9At the peril of our lives we bring in our sustenance,
   in the face of the desert heat;
10Our skin is shriveled up, as though by a furnace,
   with the searing blasts of famine.

number of letters in the Hebrew alphabet. The 3/3 meter
prevails.

1   The prayer which was lacking at the end of the previous
Lamentation is amply provided here. The poet asks Yahweh
to look upon the misfortunes which he is now going to de-
2-5 scribe. Loss of land and homes, multiplication of orphans   Ps 79:1
and widows because of the men slain in battle, paying dearly
for the necessities of life, slave labor imposed upon a people   Lam 1:11
already emaciated by hunger and weakness—all these the
poet quickly piles up before the eyes of the Lord.

6   After the Chaldean army departed, those who remained
in the country submitted for their livelihood to Egypt (to
which some, like Jeremiah, emigrated) or to the northern   Jer 43
countries, here called by their old name, Assyria.

7   The common belief in collective chastisement will be
complemented by affirming the personal guilt of the present
generation in v. 16 and during the exile by Ez 18. Jeremiah
himself saw no incompatibility between the two ideas. It was   Jer 14:20;
nonetheless true then, as today, that subsequent generations   16:10-13
must pay the price of mistakes made by previous ones, and
this was certainly true of those whose fathers perished defending Jerusalem.

8   The governors left to rule Judah are called "slaves," a term
at times used for government officials. Here it is ironic, un-
derlining the tragic reversal for a people once governed by   #1
a king.

9   Our version prefers the translation "heat" (of the desert)
for *hereb* because of the sequence and thus takes the verse
to describe the weakness with which the inhabitants of Jeru-

11The wives in Sion were ravished by the enemy.
  the maidens in the cities of Juda;
12Princes were gibbeted by them,
  elders shown no respect.
13The youths carry the millstones,
  boys stagger under their loads of wood;
14The old men have abandoned the gate,
  the young men their music.

15The joy of our hearts has ceased,
  our dance has turned into mourning;
16The garlands have fallen from our heads:
  woe to us, for we have sinned!

salem fetch food from the outlying fields in the heat of the
day. Other versions, such as the King James, Revised Stand-
ard, and Jerusalem Bible, prefer the word's other meaning,
"sword" (of the desert) and thus consider verses 9 and 10
as describing distinct woes. Bands of marauders were always
a threat to those peasants living near the edge of the desert;   Jer 6:25
in Judah's weakened state the peril became greater.

10   As in the fourth lamentation, a view is given of the raging   Lam 4:8
fever brought on by famine.

11-14   In a quick series of graphic scenes, the poet flashes before 2 Chr 36:17
the spectator's eyes each group of citizens. Women, married
and virgins, were raped by the invading armies. Princes were
hanged. Elders—who in Israelite tradition were due a religious respect — were humiliated. Youths stagger under
the loads they are made to bear. The gate, place for civic assembly, where the elders of the city made decisions
and judges held court, is abandoned; and there is no song or   Ruth 4:1
music from the young.

15-16   All joy, as Jeremiah predicted, has turned into mourning.   Jer 16:9;
The fallen garland or crown symbolizes the loss of state-   25:10
hood. For the first time in this lament, the cause is laid to   Jer 13:18
the sin of the present generation, as it was earlier to the sins   #3; 5:7;
of the fathers.   Jer 31:29f

17-18   The author of this commentary recalls visiting an abandoned and solitary tell in the Judean desert and scaring off
a jackal making its home there. The poet uses the image   Is 34:13
hyperbolically to describe the sad plight of Mount Zion, once   #1
the glory of the Judean kingdom.

19-20   Resuming the direct address, the poet reaffirms his faith   Ps 9:8;
that though Yahweh's earthly abode is demolished, he con-   45:7
tinues to reign in heaven. This article of Israelite faith be-   Ps 13:1

17Over this our hearts are sick,
  at this our eyes grow dim:
18That Mount Sion should be desolate,
  with jackals roaming there!

19You, O Lord, are enthroned forever;
  your throne stands from age to age.
20Why, then, should you forget us,
  abandon us so long a time?
21Lead us back to you, O Lord, that we may be restored:
  give us anew such days as we had of old.
22For now you have indeed rejected us,
  and in full measure turned your wrath against us.

comes the foundation of the hope in the following supplication that out of the chaos Zion's fortunes may be restored.

21   The theological climax of the entire chapter is the prayer
that Yahweh may lead his people back to him; this conver-   #3
sion is the only condition on which a restoration of pros-   Ps 80:19f
perity can be expected. The moral obligation of returning to
Yahweh and the inability to do it without his power was, in   #5
Jeremiah's interpretation, the great lesson of the fall and the   Jer 31:18f;
exile.   31:33

22   The glitter of this hope fails to diminish the anguish of
the present, and the hymn of supplication ends on a minor
chord perfectly in keeping with the mood of the entire book.

THE BOOK OF OBADIAH

Introduction

Edom and the Edomites

The occasion and the principal target of Obadiah's short prophecy are the people of Edom. A Semitic tribe, the Edomites settled in the mountains along the eastern side of the Wadi Arabah about 1300 B.C. From the 23rd to the 20th centuries this country had been the home of a florishing culture, but it was wiped out by invaders *c.* 1900 B.C. (a faint echo of which remains in the story of Abraham's battle with Chedorlaomer and his allies). For six centuries nomads roamed the country until the arrival of the Edomites, who became well established there by the time of the Exodus. In spite of the statement in Genesis that the Edomites were descended from Esau, the brother of Jacob, and thus were related to the Israelites, hostilities flared repeatedly between the two peoples. Saul fought them, David finally subdued them and gave Solomon the opportunity of developing his famous copper mines there and of shipping through the gulf of Aqabah. After the split between Israel and Judah, Edom gradually freed herself through a series of successful revolts. From then on the relations between the two peoples were a tug of war: Amaziah extended Judah's borders as far as Sela (Petra); Azariah (Uzziah) continued the march to Elath. Edom wrenched free again under Ahaz only to fall tributary to Assyria and then to Babylon in 604 B.C. When Nebuchadnezzar closed in on Jerusalem in 587 B.C., the Edomites willingly joined forces with him to avenge their ancient enemy, and after the deportation of the Judahites, they profited by the collapse to move into southern Judah, setting up their capital at Hebron. Relations do not seem to have improved after the return of the Jewish exiles from Babylon, as the Book of Obadiah indicates. In his execration of Edom the prophet reflects many of the earlier prophecies of doom upon the land of Esau, prophecies that had been written during the time of the kings when hostilities flared between the two nations. On the other hand, Obadiah says that Edom's sins against Judah are aggravated by its flaunting of the relation of brotherhood between the two (v. 10). In this he reflects the more ancient tradition according to which the two nations were identified with their eponymous ancestors, Jacob and Esau (Gn 36:1). Many features of these stories reflect the later histories of the two peoples. The name "Edom" (red), the color of the Edomite mountains, is explained either from the ruddiness of Esau or from the red color of the porridge for which he sold his birthright (Gn 25:25, 30). Mount Halak marked the southern boundary of Judah, facing Mount Seir in Edom (Jos 11:17; 12:7). Thus Jacob is described as being "smooth" (*ḥalaq*) and Esau as "hairy" (*sair*) (Gn 27:11). Deuteronomic law was relatively lenient about admitting Edomites into the community; and the author of Job makes his hero and all the characters of his drama not Judeans but Edomites (Dt 23:8). Thus the pathos we find in Obadiah reflects a phenomenon of universal human experience: the deepest hatreds are bred not between distant and unknown parties but rather between those once bound by the closest ties of kinship or friendship.

Author and occasion

The contents of Obadiah fall neatly into two parts, the dividing line being verse 15a. The first part seems to have been written at a time when the events of the fall of Jerusalem in 587 B.C. and the treacherous role of the Edomites were still fresh in the author's memory. The section bears a great similarity, even textual, with Jer 49; both passages may depend on an earlier common source. The second half is more eschatological in outlook; it speaks of the "Day of Yahweh" which is to come not only upon Edom but upon all nations and will issue in the period of Yahweh's rule from Jerusalem.

The most plausible explanation for the composition of the whole work, then, is to assume that Obadiah in the first part reworked old oracle materials against Edom—of which there was an abundance in the prophetic tradition — and then proceeded to his original contribution in the latter part (Amos 1:11-12; Ez 25:12-14; 35:1-15; Is 34:1-17).

A number of features of Obadiah indicate that he either was a temple prophet or at least wrote in the tradition of the temple prophets: use of traditional materials; allusion to a prophetic group (v. 1); the importance and centrality of Jerusalem; and particularly the theme of God's kingship from Mount Zion. "Obadiah" means "he who serves Yahweh." (In some Catholic editions of the Bible, the prophet's name is spelt "Abdia.")

Message of Obadiah

Shortest of all the prophetic books and filled with Jewish particularism, Obadiah is often scarcely noticed in a survey of the prophets. He is nonetheless witness of an important stage in the emergence of the future hope. With the great prophets he affirms Yahweh's inexorable vengeance upon the injustice of nations, aggravated in Edom's case by the violation of covenant and by her treachery against Judah, her brother-people. But beyond this, Obadiah looks to the "Day of Yahweh" when all nations will be summoned to judgment and to the day when God's kingdom will be set up on earth, fanning out from Jerusalem.

Outline of the Book of Obadiah

THE BOOK OF OBADIAH

Text and Commentary

1 The Vision of Abdia.
[Thus says the Lord God:]
Of Edom we have heard a message
from the Lord, and a herald has been sent
among the nations:
"Up! let us go to war against him!"
²See, I make you small among the nations;
you are held in dire contempt.
³The pride of your heart has deceived you:
you who dwell in the clefts of the rock,
whose abode is in the heights,
Who say in your heart,
"Who will bring me down to earth?"
⁴Though you go as high as the eagle,
and your nest be set among the stars,
From there will I bring you down,
says the Lord.

Title and prologue—1

The title, consisting of only two words, is the shortest in the
Bible. On the name Obadiah, see *Introduction*. At a moment
when a herald is being sent among the nations with an urgent
plea to form an alliance against Edom, a revelation from
Yahweh comes to the prophetic group ("we"). A revelation
by hearing, it tells how the alliance fits into God's plan concerning Edom.

Oracle against Edom—2-9

2 A favorite prophetic theme on the pride and fall of nations
is here turned against Edom. The capital of Edom was Sela,
meaning "The Rock." Situated on a high, flat-top mountain now known as *Umm-el-Bayyarah*, Sela was a natural
fortress. At its foot, in the *Wadi Musa*, the city of Petra was
later built. It is set among high, steep cliffs of Nubian sand-
stone of various shades of red. Nature itself would seem to
justify the pride of the Edomite capital. Yet even should she
build her nest higher than the eagle's, even among the stars,
5 the Lord promises to bring her down. Thieves take only

Is 14;
Jer 50—51
Ez 29—32

Jer 39:27f

5If thieves came to you, if robbers by night
  — how are you ravaged! —
  would they not steal till they had enough?
 If vintagers came to you,
  would they not leave some gleanings?
6How they search Esau,
  seek out his hiding places!
7To the border they drive you —
  all your allies;
 They deceive you, they overpower you —
  those at peace with you;
 Those who eat your bread
  lay snares beneath you:
 There is no understanding in him!
8Shall I not, says the Lord, on that day
  make the wise men disappear from Edom,
  and understanding from the mount of Esau?
9Your warriors, O Theman, shall be crushed,
  till all on Mount Esau are destroyed.
10Because of violence to your brother Jacob,
  disgrace shall cover you
  and you shall be destroyed forever.
11On the day when you stood by,
  on the day when aliens carried off his possessions,
 And strangers entered his gates

what interests them; vintage harvesters leave gleanings for the poor—an image of a remnant. But Edom's plunderers will leave nothing. Echoing the prophetic dirge that goes back to David's lament over Saul ("How they are fallen . . ."), Obadiah applies the message to the Edomites (Esau) who, rich from commerce and caravan trade, have hidden their wealth in secret recesses of the rock. They are now driven from their homeland, but less by military might than by treachery—another instance of the law of talion, for the Edomites themselves have been guilty of treachery against their fellow-nations (v. 10). Now their former allies (Hebrew, "men of your covenant"), who were at peace and had eaten the sacred covenant meal together with them, requite in kind and lay snares to trip them up. These are perhaps Arabic tribes which began to push into Edomite territory quite early, long before Petra fell to the Nabateans in 312 B.C. Edom, proverbially famous for its wise men, will be stripped of them. *Mount Esau*, an expression used only by Obadiah for the common Biblical name *Mount Seir*, is the whole Edomite mountain range extending along the Arabah. "Teman," a district of Edom, is synecdoche for the whole country.

6 Lev 19:10;
Dt 24:21
2 S 1;27
Gn 36:1

7 Is 45:3

8 Jer 49:7

and cast lots over Jerusalem,
    you too were one of them.
12Gaze not upon the day of your brother,
    the day of his disaster;
Exult not over the children of Juda
    on the day of their ruin;
Speak not haughtily
    on the day of distress!
13Enter not the gate of my people
    on the day of their calamity;
Gaze not, you at least, upon his misfortune
    on the day of his calamity;
Lay not hands upon his possessions
    on the day of his calamity!
14Stand not at the crossroads
    to slay his refugees;
Betray not his fugitives
    on the day of distress!
15For near is the day of the Lord
    for all the nations!
As you have done, so shall it be done to you,
    your deed shall come back upon your own head;

The cause—10-14

10-11 The violence is not that done by Esau to his brother Jacob Gn 25:24ff
in ancient times, but rather that of living Edomites who not
only stood idly by when the Chaldeans entered and plundered
Jerusalem in 587 but actually assisted in the operation. After
the devastation, Edom occupied the southern part of Judah.
The casting of lots was a religious rite in which the gods were
thought to direct the decision. The heinousness of the crime
was that it was done to a brother-people.

Obadiah now presses the accusation in an ironic flash-
back to the day when Edom still had the moral option of betraying or remaining loyal to his brother Judah. He pleads
with Edom not to play the traitor and thus ironically heightens the gravity of what all know now to have been the crimi-
nal decision. The accusation climaxes by recalling Edom's
waiting at the crossroads (which the Edomites knew better
than the Babylonians) to ambush the refugees. This Edom
did to his brother!

Judgment upon the nations—15-16

A new section is now begun with the introduction of the "day
of Yahweh" theme. Much of the preceding oracle was traditional material reworked by Obadiah as a background for

16As you have drunk upon my holy mountain,
  so shall all the nations drink continually.
Yes, they shall drink and swallow,
  and shall become as though they had not been.
17But on Mount Sion there shall be a portion saved;
  the mountain shall be holy,
And the house of Jacob shall take possession
  of those that dispossessed them.
18The house of Jacob shall be a fire,
  and the house of Joseph a flame;
The house of Esau shall be stubble,
  and they shall set them ablaze and devour them;
Then none shall survive of the house of Esau,
  for the Lord has spoken.
19They shall occupy the Negeb, the mount of Esau,
  and the foothills of the Philistines;
And they shall occupy the lands of Ephraim
  and the lands of Samaria,
And Benjamin shall occupy Galaad.
20The captives of this host of the children of Israel
  shall occupy the Chanaanite land as far as Sarephta,

his predictions. Now he starts afresh and looks to the coming retribution. Significantly, the "day of the Lord" concerns all nations. It will be a day of universal justice, and it is near at hand. Edom, of course, will be one of the first to experience this law of divine talion. But Judah, now addressed directly and abruptly, has already suffered her "day," the destruction of 587, when she drank of the Lord's wrath. It remains now for the rest of the nations to drink the deadly potion which will liquidate them.

Zeph 1:7, 14

16

The new kingdom of God—17-21

On Mount Zion a purified remnant will be sheltered from the awful judgment: such is the meaning of "salvation" here. the holy mount where the temple stood will be reconsecrated, and hence will be inviolable. Yahweh will manifest his living presence there once more, and from this center Judah (the house of Jacob) will repossess her lost lands, especially those of the Negeb, which the Edomites had occupied. Obadiah looks to the restoration of both the Northern and Southern Kingdoms, as Ezekiel had promised. The oracle ends with the stamp of divine authority.

Is 4:3; 37:32

17

18

Ez 25:14 Jg 9:15-20

19

The preceding oracle is now expanded by concrete geographical details: the southern desert, the mountains of Edom

> And the captives of Jerusalem who are in Sepharad
>   shall occupy the cities of the Negeb.
> 21And saviors shall ascend Mount Sion
>   to rule the mount of Esau,
>   and the kingship shall be the Lord's.

east of the Arabah, the foothills of the Philistines southwest
of Jerusalem, Samaria to the north and Gilead in northern
Transjordan — all these largely pagan districts will be incorporated into the new kingdom of God. The text of v. 20
is uncertain; it appears to mean that the captives of the
Northern Kingdom will extend the reconquest northward,
to Sarepta, a Phoenician town north of Tyre, while the captives of the Southern Kingdom will extend the boundaries
southward. Sepharad is possible Sardis, the capital of Lydia
in Asia Minor, though some scholars locate it in Media and
others in Egypt. The word "saviors" is the same used in   Jg 3:9, 15,
Judges to describe the charismatic leaders raised up by Yah-   31
weh. Here they are doubtless the line of Davidic kings, who
will once again be the mediators of God's salvation. From this
center the kingdom will extend to include the land of Edom.

Ringing out the climax to the whole prophecy, the cry,
"The kingship shall be the Lord's," merits special attention.
It is the *grande finale* of a liturgical theology centered upon
Mount Zion. In that theology, of which Obadiah is only one
among many witnesses, the reign of perfect justice and peace,
the redressment of every imbalance is called the "reign of
God." Three elements of sacramental particularism may here
be noted: (1) The center of God's rule on earth, as well
as his cult, is Jerusalem, hallowed by his dwelling-place; (2)
the Davidic king is the mediator of this reign; (3) the remnant of faithful Israelites are the beneficiaries and the in-
struments of this restoration. For the Christian, these elements were conclusively fulfilled only in Jesus Christ, the
Davidic Messiah who shed his blood in the Holy City and   Acts 1:6-8
reconsecrated a remnant who from Mount Zion extended
God's kingdom to all the world.

The margin numbers: 20, 21

Passages used as Readings in the Breviary

Zeph	1:1-9	Wednesday in the fifth week of November
	3:8-13	Canticle during Easter Time
Na	1:1-10	Monday in the fifth week of November
Hb	1:1-10	Tuesday in the fifth week of November
	3:2-10	Canticle on Friday and various feasts
Lam	1:1-14	Holy Thursday
	1:2, 20-21; 2:13, 15-18	Feast of Seven Sorrows, September 15
	2:8-15; 3:1-9	Good Friday
	3:22-30; 4:1-5; 5:1-11	Holy Saturday
	5:1-7, 15-17, 19-21	Canticle during Lent
Ob	1:1-11	Friday in the fourth week of November

Passages used in the Weekday Lectionary

Zephaniah 1:14-18; 2:1-3 Thursday in the Last Week after Pentecost
Habakkuk 3:3-19 Wednesday in the Last Week after Pentecost

ABBREVIATIONS

Gn—Genesis	Wis—Wisdom	Lk—Luke
Ex—Exodus	Sir—Sirach	Jn—John
Lv—Leviticus	Is—Isaiah	Acts—Acts
Nm—Numbers	Jer—Jeremiah	Rom—Romans
Dt—Deuteronomy	Lam—Lamentations	1 Cor—1 Corinthians
Jos—Joshua	Bar—Baruch	2 Cor—2 Corinthians
Jg—Judges	Ez—Ezekiel	Gal—Galatians
Ruth—Ruth	Dn—Daniel	Eph—Ephesians
1 S—1 Samuel	Hos—Hosea	Phil—Philippians
2 S—2 Samuel	Jl—Joel	Col—Colossians
1 K—1 Kings	Amos—Amos	1 Th—1 Thessalonians
2 K—2 Kings	Ob—Obadiah	2 Th—2 Thessalonians
1 Chr—1 Chronicles	Jon—Jonah	1 Tim—1 Timothy
2 Chr—2 Chronicles	Mi—Micah	2 Tim—2 Timothy
Ezr—Ezra	Na—Nahum	Tit—Titus
Neh—Nehemiah	Hb—Habakkuk	Phm—Philemon
Tob—Tobit	Zeph—Zephaniah	Heb—Hebrews
Jud—Judith	Hg—Haggai	Jas—James
Est—Esther	Zech—Zechariah	1 Pt—1 Peter
Jb—Job	Mal—Malachi	2 Pt—2 Peter
Ps—Psalms	1 Mac—1 Maccabees	1 Jn—1 John
Prv—Proverbs	2 Mac—2 Maccabees	2 Jn—2 John
Qoh—Qoheleth	Mt—Matthew	3 Jn—3 John
Ct—Canticles	Mk—Mark	Jude—Jude
		Ap—Apocalypse

ANET—*Ancient Near Eastern Texts* edited by James B. Pritchard (Princeton University Press, Princeton, New Jersey)

REVIEW AIDS AND DISCUSSION TOPICS

I.

Introduction to Zephaniah *pages* 3-9

1. Describe Manasseh's Assyrian Policy. Why did he silence the prophets?
2. What do we know about Zephaniah?
3. Does most of his book fit the historical context of the regency?
4. Discuss his message and theology, explaining his use of cosmic imagery, "the fire of God's jealousy," the *'anawim.*
5. Develop the topics in an outline of the book of Zephaniah.

II.

Text and exegesis of the book of Zephaniah *pages* 10-23

1. How does Zephaniah describe the Day of the Lord? Will any escape God's searching judgment?
2. Who were the Philistines? What is their role in the history of the people of God?
3. Summarize the oracles against Moab and Ammon, Egypt, Assyria, Jerusalem.
4. How does the universalism of judgment melt into a universalism of mercy?
5. Discuss some of the New Testament contacts with the last chapters of this book.

III.

Introduction to Nahum *pages* 24-28

1. What is the historical setting for the book of Nahum?
2. Why was the short oracle of Zephaniah (2:13-15) expanded in this book?
3. What was the occasion and date of this book? Define a "salvation oracle."
4. What is the message of Nahum?
5. What does archaeology say about this book? Outline its contents.

IV.

Text and exegesis of the book of Nahum *pages* 29-44

1. Discuss the opening theophany (1:2-10) and its insistence on God's wrath.
2. What is the meaning of the oracles addressed to Judah and Assyria?
3. Describe the attack on Nineveh.
4. What is the theological significance of Nineveh's downfall?
5. How does Nahum develop the themes: blood, lies, plunder in his final description of the collapse of the city?

V.

Introduction to Habakkuk *pages* 45-47

1. What is the historical problem of the book of Habakkuk?
2. What is the cultic solution of this problem?
3. What answers does he give to the question: Why do the wicked flourish and the just suffer?
4. How does Paul develop this theme: "The just man by his fidelity will live?
5. Of what value to exegetes is the Qumran scroll of Habakkuk? Outline the contents of this book.

VI.

Text and exegesis of the book of Habakkuk *pages* 48-62

1. How does Habakkuk call God to account? What response does the Lord give?
2. Why does the prophet make a second complaint?
3. Discuss the implications of the words: just, faith, life in the Lord's second answer.
4. How did Paul understand these words?
5. Summarize the five woes addressed to the oppressor. Show how the canticle in 3:1-19 is a perfect climax to the preceding chapters.

VII.

Lamentations *pages* 63-97

1. What are the difficulties in admitting that Jeremiah is the author of Lamentations? Give examples of the qinah meter, the acrostic form in this book.
2. What is the theological message and the significance of Lamentations?
3. Name and discuss the eight dominant motifs of this book.
4. How is the first lamentation divided? What is the final message of faith? How does the second lamentation develop the theme of tragic reversal? Point out some of the differences between the third lamentation and the others.
5. Show how the fourth lamentation closely resembles the second. Why is the fifth lamentation more correctly entitled "A national prayer for God's mercy in the sense both of forgiveness and restoration?"

VIII.

Obadiah *pages* 98-105

1. Outline the history of Edom. How are some of the ancient traditions of these people reflected in the Bible?
2. What do we know about the author of this book?
3. What is the occasion and the message of these 21 verses?
4. How does this message compare with Ps 137?
5. Why are the words, "The kingship shall be the Lord's, a fitting climax to the whole prophecy? Could you isolate a theme underlying all the prophetic oracles in this booklet?